Michael Whitehall worked as a journalist, preparatory schoolmaster, solicitor's articled clerk, charity fundraiser, copywriter and public relations consultant before becoming a theatrical agent and television and theatre producer. He appeared with his son Jack in BBC2's *Backchat* and *Travels with My Father* for Netflix, and has finally achieved his lifetime ambition of sitting in 'Dictionary Corner' on Channel 4's *Countdown*. He lives in London.

Backing into the Spotlight

Michael Whitehall

CONSTABLE

CONSTABLE

First published in Great Britain in 2017 by Constable
This paperback edition published in 2018

1 3 5 7 9 10 8 6 4 2

A CIP catalogue record for this book
is available from the British Library.

ISBN: 978-1-47212-708-2

Typeset in Sabon LT by Hewer Text UK Ltd, Edinburgh
Printed and bound in Great Britain by Clays Ltd, Elcograf S.p.A.

Papers used by Constable are from well-managed
forests and other responsible sources.

Constable
An imprint of
Little, Brown Book Group
Carmelite House
50 Victoria Embankment
London EC4Y 0DZ

An Hachette UK Company
www.hachette.co.uk

www.littlebrown.co.uk

For Hilary, Jack, Molly and Barney

Contents

Foreword

I think my father had originally planned to write a book about Winston Churchill, whom he idolised for getting him through the last war virtually unscathed; although he has a few unresolved mental issues about being born in 1940, like an obsession with Nazi memorabilia and numerous books on Adolf Hitler. He even uses a metal statue of Mussolini as a doorstop to his study, which is pretty weird.

Anyway, I did a bit of research into this Churchill book idea and discovered that tens of thousands of books have been written about Winston and that a market that crowded would certainly not have room for another one, especially when it was written not by a distinguished historian but by a retired theatrical agent and ex-Deputy Chairman of the Putney Common Association.

My father then announced his 'Plan B': an autobiography.

'A lot of people have asked me why I haven't written a sequel to *Shark Infested Waters*,' he said.

I wondered who these people were.

'People,' he said. 'Neil Stacy, Hilary, Antonia Wainman . . .'

'Your best friend, your wife and your dog walker . . . a very unbiased sample. So you honestly think that ordinary people are going to be rushing into bookshops, not to buy Patricia Cornwell's latest bestseller, or the new Robert Harris, or Barack Obama's autobiography, but another book by seventy-seven-year-old Michael Whitehall? I wouldn't bother!'

Six months later, my father arranged to meet me at The Garrick Club. When I arrived, the porter asked if he could help me.

'I'm meeting my father here,' I replied.

He looked me up and down, checking my clean Stan Smith trainers, smart black skinny jeans, plaid shirt and tailored leather jacket.

'Not dressed like that you're not,' he said as he gestured for me to step back onto the pavement.

'You're in good company,' said my father, when he finally arrived to find me standing in the street. 'I read that the same thing happened to One Direction the other evening, when they allegedly went into a smart club, only to be ejected by the doorman with a firm "the only direction you're going is out of the door".'

We went to a bar up the street, where, over a Hendricks and tonic, my father asked me to write this foreword.

'A foreword to what?' I asked him.

'My book,' he replied.

'I don't know anything about Winston Churchill, other than that he drunk Pol Roger champagne, smoked Havana cigars and stayed in bed until midday.'

'No, I took your advice and dumped my Churchill book idea and went for a book about my life and career.'

I was speechless. My advice had been not to write either book; advice as ever that he studiously chose to ignore.

So I read it. I have to admit that my father has made rather a good job of it. I just have a couple of quibbles, not least the title. I don't know about *Backing into the Spotlight*, a more accurate one would be *Crowbarring Myself into the Spotlight*.

And of course I have heard all these stories before, many times.

The word 'semi' should definitely be attached to autobiography, as he is wont to exaggerate and I'm not sure that all of them are strictly true. But to use the old adage, my father has never been one to let the truth get in the way of a good story.

In any case it's a further glimpse into the world of Michael Whitehall and will make an excellent stocking filler . . . but wait until Christmas 2018 when it will almost certainly have been remaindered.

Jack

Prologue

The *Oldie* Lunch, 2007

'The only people you see in bookshops these days are writers moving their books around,' said Craig Brown to his virgin writer friend. 'It's essential that you're on one of the tables and not on the shelves.'

It had already occurred to me that being 'on the shelves' was pretty hopeless, especially if your name began with a W. To see, let alone reach, a W book, involved lying on your stomach in a dark corner, trying to focus on a clutch of W, X, Y and Z titles, usually bunched far too closely together. Not a problem Craig Brown ever encountered. I wonder how well Franco Zeffirelli's autobiography sold?

I had been invited to speak at an *Oldie* literary lunch at Simpson's-in-the-Strand.

'Drinks, lunch, talk for a maximum of fifteen minutes about your book and then signing,' said Richard Ingrams firmly.

He introduced me to Earl Spencer, who was one of the other speakers.

'Everyone seems to be really disappointed – they thought I was Charles Spencer the theatre critic.'

'Ingrams has given me a lousy seat at the far end of the table,' said Peter McKay of the *Daily Mail*.

'That's because you never replied to the invitation,' said Ingrams.

'What's Michael Whitehall doing on the top table?' asked McKay. 'He's an agent. Have you ever eaten with an agent?'

I sat next to Charles Spencer during lunch, while McKay scowled up at us from the Siberian end of the table. He tried to get his own back the following day by writing a scurrilous piece in his column, saying that Earl Spencer dyed his hair.

After the speeches, we signed our books. The Earl had a long snaking queue of dowagers holding open their copies of *Prince Rupert: The Last Cavalier* for him to sign. One beckoned to him conspiratorially and whispered, 'May I just say . . . that speech . . . in the Abbey . . . you spoke for us all.'

And another: 'Did you write all this yourself?'

'The two most common questions I get asked,' he told me as the ladies wandered off chatting to each other.

'What a charming young man,' I heard one of them say.

'Old Etonian, of course.'

Meanwhile the queue to my left for Christopher Robbins's *In Search of Kazakhstan* was building nicely, leaving a rather embarrassing gap in front of me.

'Is *Shark Infested Waters* your first book?' enquired a red-faced man in a Garrick Club tie who had drifted out of the Spencer queue and looked as though he'd given the Simpson's vin de table quite a hammering.

'Yes, it is actually,' I replied.

'Emma Chizzet,' he slurred.

'Emma who?'

'Sorry, very old joke,' he said. 'How much is it?'

'Oh, erm . . . £16.99.'

'But that's only two pounds less than Spencer's book, and he's a proper writer and Princess Diana's brother, for God's sake.'

'Yes, well, I'm sorry about that,' I said as he drifted off into the room in search of another glass of wine.

The following day I flew up to Edinburgh to see my son Jack, who was appearing at the Festival Fringe. Killing time in Princes Street, I wandered into Waterstones, which had a large window display of *Prince Rupert* and details of its author's appearance at the Literary Festival that evening. The prominent centre table was awash with his book, but sadly no copies of *Shark Infested Waters* were in evidence.

'You might find it in Marine Wildlife on the second floor,' said an eager young assistant.

I found it in Biographies on the first floor, in the bottom right-hand corner of a large bookcase – four copies squeezed in between Terry Venables and Dale Winton. The nearby table was piled high with books, but I spotted one potential gap, currently occupied by a single volume of Michael Winner's memoir. Never a man to bear grudges, I ceased to be a fan as a result of being the target of some aggressive bullying from Mr Winner, a renowned egotist and vexatious litigant, aimed at several of my clients. I removed the book, tucked it under the table and started to transfer *Shark Infested Waters*, one book at a time, from the shelf to the table. As I was carefully placing the fourth copy on top of the third, a stern voice behind me said, 'Can I help you sir?'

I'd been rumbled.

I turned sheepishly round.

'I know exactly what you're up to, Mr Whitehall,' said Earl Spencer.

1

How Did I Get Here?

Standing in front of a full-length mirror in my dressing room at the ITV Studios in 2013, waiting to go on to the set of *Backchat*, dressed in a sequinned jacket and gloves, a full-length white faux-fur coat and a pink cowboy hat, I had a brief conversation with my reflection.

'Michael, what the fuck do you think you're doing?'

When Jack and I were filming *Backchat* with Nick Hewer as one of our guests, not the one involving the costume above, I hasten to add, Jack told him that my greatest aspiration in life was to appear in 'Dictionary Corner' on *Countdown*. As is often the case with Jack, this was a slight exaggeration, but it fitted his narrative with regards to my onscreen character, a bad-tempered old fart who spends his life reading *The Times* and the *Spectator*, and watching *The Antiques Roadshow* and *Countdown*. Whenever I described my persona on *Backchat* as an exaggeration of myself, Jack would always contradict me and say that there was no exaggeration of any kind. I remember on one occasion, at a production meeting in the ITV studios on the South Bank, he was listing what he deemed to be my worst excesses.

'You're an outrageous, bigoted, ridiculous, right-wing, snobby, *Telegraph*-reading, Trump-loving, racist, misogynist, xenophobic Brexiteer.'

I put him straight back into his basket.

'How dare you!' I said. 'That is a vicious lie! You know perfectly well that I have never, in my entire life, read any newspaper other than *The Times*!'

When I was growing up in suburban Beckenham, I have to admit that I was a bit of a show-off. My brother Barry was the polar opposite. While I was embarrassing my parents' guests with a semi-spontaneous mime to Buddy Holly's 'That'll be the Day', a reluctant Barry would act as director and lighting designer, shining a table lamp in my face and holding back the living-room curtains while I performed.

I was also very into modern jazz at the time, and would mime to an instrumental track, pretending to play the trumpet, saxophone, piano, bass and drums. I would occasionally perform in front of a mirror, but more often in front of my long-suffering parents, Jack and Nora, who found the whole process alarming. Basically, I was making up for the fact that I couldn't actually sing or play any musical instrument, and this was the best I had to offer. I had a fruitless period of learning to play the piano from a monk at Ampleforth, I think his name was Father Boniface, who clearly had only a passing interest in music, and a very short fuse when it came to wrong notes, which I offered him in abundance. To say 'learning to play' was a misnomer: I learnt nothing, and to this day can only bang out the first six chords of Tchaikovsky's Piano Concerto No. 1 and half of 'Chopsticks'. I was always late for my lessons and did no practice between them.

Hard on the heels of Barry giving up the violin, in my opinion definitely a very good call, Nora was even more devastated when I gave up the piano. Nora had such high aspirations for us; she was a modestly talented pianist herself, and hoped that one day we would play duets together, possibly at the Royal Albert Hall, but this sadly never came to pass. I then took up the drums, which I thought would be an easier option, as indeed it proved to be. As I was never going to master a musical instrument, why not play an instrument that required no boring scales and arpeggios, with neither practice nor skill, apart from the ability to bang them at the right time and in the right order? I always overdid the cymbal. I had a brief period of being in charge of the timpani department in the Ampleforth school orchestra, a role given to me more out of sympathy than admiration of my talent. I was also a particularly dab hand at the triangle, although I did find it quite arduous, not to say boring, counting two hundred and forty-two bars' rest to then 'ting' it twice. On one occasion, during a lapse in concentration, I hit the cymbal rather than the triangle, causing havoc to what had previously been a rather impressive performance of Schubert's Unfinished Symphony, in front of an appreciative audience of parents and staff. I decided at that point that the Royal College of Music should probably come off my wish list.

As I had been such a disappointment to my mother, I wanted to instil a love of music into my children. The words 'Tiger Dad' have often been applied to me; certainly I considered it to be my role as a father to introduce them to the joys of fine art and music. OK, I had given Schubert's Unfinished Symphony a finish it had never had before, but little else on my musical CV showed such originality. So it was time for me to have a second chance through my children. Jack played the recorder from an early age and appeared on stage in a wind ensemble of eight-year-olds at Tower House School in East Sheen, although in reality the sound emanating from the ensemble had more in common with wind of another kind. But, like his father, he found practising the recorder tiresome. I was reluctant to cough up for 'extra' music lessons when all Jack did was pretend that his recorder was a light sabre and that he was Luke Skywalker. True, he was a late developer, but doing that aged sixteen was quite worrying.

With my help, Molly chose the cello – such an appropriate instrument for her, I thought at the time. I have always been a huge fan and admirer of the late Jacqueline du Pré and I saw many similarities between her and Molly. Long hair, graceful hands and the elegant way in which she held her bow. Unfortunately, Molly was a particularly petite child, and the choice of the cello turned out to be a bad call as she was forced to cart the bloody thing up and down Putney Hill on her way to school a couple of days a week. Unlike her brother, she did practise it regularly, but unfortunately, despite holding the bow so elegantly, when it came into contact with the strings, the sound was more shrill than mellow, reminiscent of Bernard Herrmann's excellent music track to the shower scene in Alfred Hitchcock's *Psycho*. She gave it up when she developed back trouble, which impacted on her performances in the gym squad; that seemed far more important to her than my aspirations of her becoming a world-famous cellist.

And then there was Barney, who had never shown any interest whatsoever in matters musical, and suddenly announced one day out of the blue that he wanted to play the oboe. Now the oboe is not an easy instrument to master, and indeed he didn't disappoint in that department. But he was very conscientious about practising. He even insisted on extra practice whenever the practice room was available. However, he was eventually nailed by his oboe teacher, Miss Pratchett, who suspected, due to his lack of progress, that he was probably up to something else. One afternoon she positioned herself outside the door of the practice room and waited. After a few silent minutes, she opened the door and discovered that the window had been flung open and Barney had disappeared to join his mates playing football. Oboe lessons ceased from then on.

Whenever we met the school librarian, Mrs Grosvenor, a lady in her early sixties, she would always tell us what a charming boy Barney was and how much she enjoyed her weekly chats with him.

'He's such an avid reader with such wide tastes in literature,' she said. 'And he's always so prompt at returning books to the library every week and picking out a new one. So many children hang on to books for weeks and weeks, preventing others from borrowing them.' Now this news came as quite a surprise to his mother and me, as we had never actually seen Barney open a book in his life. The bookcase in his bedroom contained a few old Arsenal programmes, the odd Marvel comic and some magazines under his bed, which were light on literary content but heavy pictorially, and which Barney said, when they were discovered by our cleaning lady Regina, that he was looking after for Jack while he was away on holiday. It turned out that Barney hadn't actually been reading any of these books. He genuinely liked chatting with Mrs Grosvenor, and of course it helped that there was always a good supply of chocolate digestives in her biscuit tin, but the truth was that the top floor of the library was the ideal place to hide and play Football Manager with his friends, without fear of discovery.

Barney was often in close proximity to trouble, and usually of his own making. He was clearly an admirer of The Nigel Havers School Of Life, whereby you can go a long way and get yourself out of most scrapes by deploying the 'c' bomb – *charm*. Although it failed miserably on one occasion, when Barney made a particularly bad judgement call during his mock GCSEs and found himself in some very hot water. He was waiting to go into his physics exam and chatting with his friend Tarquin, who said that he had forgotten to bring his calculator with him. Barney smelt an opportunity.

'If I lend you my calculator, will you do the calculations and we'll share the answers?' asked Barney. He knew that Tarquin was better at physics than him, so he was going to get the better end of the deal.

Three days later, both boys were called into the frosty senior master's study. He told them that there was a major problem with their physics papers.

'Both of you have done very poorly in your exam, which came as no surprise, but more puzzlingly, you have the same mark.' He paused. 'You have identical wrong answers, particularly the answer to the question "Explain the shape of the graph", where you have both literally described the shape of the graph, rather than what the shape means. Can either of you explain this?' They were both given a fixed suspension or, in real terms, had a ton of bricks thrown at them. To be honest, the only A grade Barney was going to get near was in smoking behind The Charcoal Grill, a kebab shop in Marlborough High Street.

He did have one moment of glory at school, however, when he was ten and cast as Joseph in *Joseph and the Amazing Technicolour Dreamcoat*. At last, this was the Whitehall family's chance to make an impact on the world of music and opera. In truth, popular musicals came well down my wish list, and certainly would not have registered on Nora's cultural radar, but fortunately I had several contacts in that world, who were alerted regarding Barney's upcoming performance – Sir Tim Rice, Sir Andrew Lloyd Webber, Sir Cameron Mackintosh and a former client, film and West End theatre star, Petula Clarke. My wife Hilary filmed the show and sent them all a copy, but sadly they were all returned unopened; rather typical of that end of the business!

Barney was blessed with a beautiful singing voice but disappointingly, despite a fine vocal range, he had absolutely no interest in performing. This, coupled with the fact that some of the older boys had told him after a rehearsal one day that he sounded like a *castrato* – and that it was 'not cool' to be good at singing – meant he became a very reluctant leading man. The singing element of his performance was outstanding; so much so that he collected a fan club of younger girls, who used to follow behind him down the school corridors, giggling if he smiled at them. It was at this time that Barney's older brother, always game for a cheap laugh even then, gave Barney the nickname Smoocher, subsequently shortened to Smooch, which has stuck with him ever since. But the passages in between the songs were less successful, as Barney stood with hands in pockets, hopping from foot to foot, clearly not wanting to be there and yawning when he was not the centre of attention. So we knew early on that a career in show business was probably not for him.

Molly fared better on the performing front, being cast in various leading parts in school productions, and also appeared in a couple of television programmes that I produced. But being pretty savvy, she quickly realised that the advice received by Mrs Worthington about life on the stage was probably sound, so there would be no show-business career for her, whereas Jack, of course, lurched straight into show business, having had a brief flirtation with art.

I had made several unremarkable appearances in various school plays. My Gremio, in an all-male production of *The Taming of The Shrew* (I auditioned for Kate, but without success) was well received, but led only to my being overlooked for other productions. The monk in charge of drama told me, rather spitefully I thought, that I spent far too much time looking at the audience rather than at my fellow performers, so I spent my remaining time at school in the prompt corner. From where, on one occasion, I had to leave rather suddenly for a toilet break, and upon my return found myself in the middle of a hornet's nest, as the actor playing Juliet had dried, and had asked for a prompt three times, before Romeo had had to step in with the line, causing loud bursts of laughter from the audience.

So a life in show business was certainly not for me. I had absolutely no idea what I wanted to do, but I learnt through experience what I didn't want to do, via a string of jobs during my twenties including film critic of *The Universe,* a shelf stacker at Oakeshotts in Sloane Street, private tutor to the son of Greville Wynne, the British spy imprisoned in the Soviet Union and ultimately released, a salesman for an export and import company in East London, a bar student of the Middle Temple, an articled clerk at the Crown solicitors Williams & James in Gray's Inn, teaching English in a north London language school for foreign students, a PR consultant in Bond Street, a copywriter in a West End advertising agency, a preparatory schoolmaster (three times), a charity fundraiser for The National Association of Boys' Clubs and London social secretary to the singer and entertainer Tiny Tim, finally landing up in an actors' agency.

I had absolutely no idea what an actors' agent actually did, and I assumed it would be another short-term engagement; although, who knows, having not achieved high-end status in anything so far, maybe I could look after high-end actors instead? Little did I know that I would still be at it forty years later. At no point in those forty years did I ever hanker after being in front of the camera. I was very happy to be in the shadows, to the extent that when offered the opportunity to swap sides, I didn't. In 1980 Michael Grade very generously and totally inaccurately told me that I was the funniest man in London, and would I be interested in taking over the slot left vacant at London Weekend Television by the defection of Russell Harty to the BBC and having my own chat show? This was an enquiry rather than an offer, of course, but I didn't give it a moment's thought.

Why would I want to stop being an agent, with a rising salary, and put my head above the parapet and become a performer? Absolutely no way.

So how did I find myself thirty-five years later, standing in that dressing room, dripping in sequins?

2

'Is Anything Happening?'

I was an actors' agent for over forty-five years, working at London International, IFA, ICM, Leading Artists and, finally, Whitehall Artists. The first three were in fact the same agency, which kept changing its name – confusing for both agents and clients. There was a joke around at the time among our American colleagues; they suggested that because we English agents were so spineless and cowardly, when it came to getting rid of unwanted clients, we couldn't get rid of them to their face – we could only do it by changing the name of the agency and moving buildings.

I was twenty-nine when I began agenting, and seventy-five when I finished. I probably looked after several hundred actors and actresses (we used to be allowed to call them 'actresses' in those days), several directors and an Oscar-winning director of photography. Most of my clients were male, for no particular reason; it just worked out that way. Unlike a small but distinguished agent of the 1970s, whose assistant I briefly was, who never looked after actresses. 'Very difficult people, actresses,' he told me. 'Most of them have huge egos, are very needy and have a totally unmerited opinion of their own talent. And, worst of all, the reflection they see in the mirror is of a woman half their age.'

I remember being asked to 'look after and extend all courtesies to' Dorothy Lamour by her US agent during a trip she made to London. When I met Miss Lamour, best known for playing Bob Hope and Bing Crosby's love interest in several of their 'Road' pictures, at Heathrow, I wasn't expecting the apparition that materialised in the arrivals hall, struggling with her suitcases and resembling someone who was awaiting the delivery of a wheelchair. Now in her mid-sixties, she looked twenty years older. In the taxi on the way to her hotel she explained that, although she was in London primarily to see friends, she'd like me to line up some meetings for her with producers and casting directors. She became rather upset when I broached the topic of her 'playing age'.

'I play forty,' she said very firmly, which produced a loud guffaw from our cab driver.

'I saw you in the *The Jungle Princess*, Miss Lamour,' he said. 'My parents took me to see it when I was a child,' he added with a wry smile. (I'd never heard of *The Jungle Princess*, but when I checked it out I saw that it had been released in 1936.) She was also concerned that she might clash with Julie Christie, whom the agency also represented, even though Julie Christie was born in 1940 and she was born in 1914.

'Dorothy Lamour?' said Maude Spector, doyenne of casting directors. 'I didn't realise she was still with us.'

The only meeting I managed to get for her was to play Miss Haversham, described by her creator Charles Dickens as 'a cross between a waxwork and a skeleton', in a TV adaptation of *Great Expectations*. She declined to attend the meeting and returned to the States a fortnight later without even saying goodbye.

So I think that notion must have stuck in my mind, subliminally somewhere, as I always had a male-dominated list; although I did have some success with a few actresses I represented, Dorothy Tutin, Angela Thorne and Irene Handl, a consummate character actress, who I looked after for many years. When she was rehearsing a play at the National Theatre, the director, an intense and humourless man, tried to have a deep and meaningful conversation with Irene about the text over lunch one day.

'I'm sorry my love,' said Irene, as she tucked into a cheese and chutney sandwich, 'but I think you must be confusing me with someone who gives a fuck.'

I was, however, strongly advised not to take on married couples.

'They're very competitive with one another,' my boss at London International, Laurie Evans, told me, clearly with the benefit of bitter experience. 'And when you call them with an offer, the wrong one *always* answers the phone and you have to make small talk until you pluck up the courage to ask for their other half.'

I also looked after a male gay couple in the late 1970s, which didn't work out either because they bickered with each other all the time. Being of a similar age, they were hugely competitive to the point that, on one occasion, after I had arranged – with some difficulty – a meeting for one of them with a top TV director, the other one insisted on going to the meeting with his partner, prompting him as he read and even suggesting himself for his partner's part. Predictably, the director was not impressed, and neither of them was cast, so I quickly let them go to a more relaxed and sympathetic agent.

Sympathy with the plight of my clients was not my strong suit. I thought my role was to be a ruthless negotiator, who would stop at nothing to get his clients the very best deal. I heard (many years after Richard Griffiths came to me) that he had toured around various producers, asking them which agent was the most annoying, the one that they hated having to deal with most. Following this research, he asked me to take him on! I felt it was very important to keep a clear division between my business and social life; other agents were

my competitors, and being chums with casting directors would muddy the waters when I found myself
trying to hammer out a good deal. So I would avoid at
all costs cosy lunches or after-work drinks with fellow
agents or casting directors.

This approach was vindicated when I appeared in the
Chancery Division of the High Court in a case brought
by my ex-girlfriend (now referred to in legal texts as
Windeler v. Whitehall), who was looking for a share of
my house and business, or a 'beneficial interest' to quote
the correct legal term. Mr Justice Millet, in summing up
(in my favour, I'm pleased to say), in referring to the
suggestion that getting and keeping clients involved
high-end wining-and-dining 24/7 and not much else,
said:

'Only a schoolgirl would think that the life of a theatrical agent was glamorous, or that he acquired his
clientele by maintaining a high social profile. I think she
had very little idea of what Mr Whitehall actually did in
the office or the tedium and hard grind that in fact the
job involves.'

Tedium and hard grind? Well, maybe not quite that
bad; though I was always prepared to grind out a good
deal.

In his seminal book, *Adventures in The Screen Trade*,
William Goldman said that 'being an agent is all about

signing clients'. Laurie Evans told me exactly the same, but was furious with me when, within a year of becoming his assistant, I had heeded his advice and taken on two of his own clients. As I told him, I had learnt from one of the best, so he shouldn't have been surprised when his advice came back to bite him.

After a few months of sucking up to him and keeping my hands off his clients, I was given the ultimate accolade, shared only by one other employee, of a key to his private cloakroom on the top floor of our offices in Hanover Square. Positioned outside Laurie's room, my own key was a major step up the corporate ladder for me; though it thoroughly pissed off Laurie's other assistant, Michael Linnett, who had been in place as the heir apparent well ahead of me, but who still hadn't got his hands on a key to the Holy of Holies.

To describe Laurie's loo as lavish would be an understatement. The oak door with a brass plaque saying 'PRIVATE' was Yale-locked and awash with Roger & Gallet soaps, thick Hermès towels and assorted men's fragrances. The loo paper was thick and quilted, and Laurie made sure that it was cleaned every day by our very relaxed Spanish cleaning lady Maria. In contrast the main office lavatory in the basement, which I had used up to this point, had a roller towel, usually empty, so we dried our hands on the net curtains that covered the light well, a bar of cracked soap and shiny loo paper. Maria seldom visited this room and it was not a place to linger in.

There was one particular actor I was keen to represent. Let's call him Alec. I knew him reasonably well and I suspected he might be looking for a change of agent. He and his then wife had split up and he was at a loose end. I was pretty free and loose-endish at the time, too, as my then girlfriend, the one I ended up in the High Court with, was crewing on round-the-world yachts for most of the year, which is maybe why our relationship ended up on the rocks. So Alec and I started hanging out in the evenings together. A few early drinks, a spot of dinner somewhere and then perhaps a club, Annabel's or Crockfords maybe. Quite a bit of drink flowed through the evenings, although I did draw the line at any sexual adventures. (My girlfriend may have been sailing around the Horn of Africa, but I kept my horns to myself.) But I was eating and drinking far too much and getting to bed far too late, although it was all in a good cause, I thought.

Most of our chat up to this point was gossipy, with obviously a lot of talk about his career, always a favoured topic when spending time with an actor. And then, one morning, following a late supper at The Garrick Club and more than a couple of large Kümmels, I decided it was time to move in on my quarry and broach the question of his representation. I planned to tell him that evening that I would love not just to be his friend but also his agent, and that I knew this could be a hugely profitable relationship for us both. I would also add that his current agent was over the hill and that he needed a younger man to take his career on to the next level. Before I headed to Langan's Brasserie to meet him for dinner, I had a call from a producer friend of mine. After the usual pleasantries, he told me that he had talked to Alec earlier in the day and my name had come up. Alec's view was clear: he was bloody pleased I wasn't his agent.

'Michael is very entertaining and I'm very fond of him, but I'd hate him to be my agent. He's out every night eating and drinking, sometimes well into the small hours. He must be shot to bits when he gets to his office!'

Despite this setback, I continued on my quest to expand the client list. I was at a party in Richmond, which was awash with young actors and actresses, several of whom I was anxious to have on my books. One actor in particular I had heard was unhappy with his agent and ready for a change, and as I was about to break into his conversation with a glamorous young actress and tell him how wonderful he was in his current West End play, I was almost knocked sideways by a young man. He had clearly given his host's champagne a good hammering and, as he prodded me in the chest, he announced rather too loudly: 'I've heard all about you, you're going to be my new agent!'

At that point I had no idea who he was, other than that Kenneth More was a good friend of his father, Michael Havers, who was then the Attorney General. So a quick call to Kenny the following day revealed that he was very promising and I should give him a chance despite his rather unconventional approach. So Nigel Havers came on board, followed by several other actors of similar provenance joining him on my list, such as Ian Ogilvy, Simon Williams and Christopher Cazenove. A 'Cluster of Toffs', someone referred to them as.

It's always a difficult call for an actor. Do they want to be with an agent who has several similar clients, so if one isn't free for a job, another one will be? Or do they want to be his one and only of a particular type? In my time I had a few other 'clusters' on my books: a Skulk of Foxes, Edward, his wife Joanna David, his daughter Emilia and his brother James; a Pride of Davenports, Nigel, his wife Maria Aitken and their son Jack. But I soon realised that, despite what they said, actors don't really like to share the same agent as their friends and relatives. A doctor or accountant maybe, but an agent or a personal manager – as some agents grandly call themselves – is for their personal use only.

Certainly the last thing actors want is to hear about your other clients. You just don't talk about them. The American actress Ethel Merman once said, 'If you ain't

21

talkin' about me, I ain't listenin.' Otherwise you could fall into one of two traps:

Trap 1: Trying to cheer up your out-of-work actor by telling him/her that most of your other clients are out of work too. Wrong! If they are all out of work, what hope have you got of landing a job?

Trap 2: Trying to cheer up your out-of-work actor by telling him/her that most of your other clients are working. Wrong! Great, so he's got them jobs but not me?

Another universal truth that all agents must live with every day of their lives is that clients will sometimes leave them. I had my fair share of departures – some expected, some not. When an actor is doing well, it's all his own doing, but when he isn't getting any work, or isn't getting the right kind of work, or is generally just pissed off with the actor's life, there isn't really anything he can do about it, other than sack his agent . . .

Richard E. Grant went from, 'I thank God every day that I met you and you took me on' to, 'I'm afraid I just don't know who to believe any more, so I am moving on', following an introduction he'd been given to what I thought was a particularly bullshitting and predatory American agent (is there any other kind?). I was sacked by him, the circumstances of which I covered in some detail in Chapter 9 of my first book, *Shark Infested Waters*, entitled 'They Come, They Go,

Who Called?', and which Jack covered in Chapter 19, entitled 'Dirty Den', of our jointly written book, *Him and Me*. So, I have no intention of re-telling the story here for the third time, as it was of no importance to me then, nor indeed now. It was of no consequence, and I probably won't refer to it ever again, unless – I suppose – if I were to write another book. Colin Firth left me after several successful years together because, as he explained to a mutual friend, he didn't get my sense of humour and never knew when I was joking. Years later, when we met at a party, he said, 'I think I could cope with you now.'

Then there were those who came, then went, then came back again, despite my policy of *never* taking back a client who had left me. The charming and urbane Simon Williams left me, came back and then left me again and, despite ruining a rare family holiday in Barbados by having me grafted to a fax machine in ninety-degree heat in the office of our hotel, sorting out a contractual horror story that he was embroiled in, we still remain good friends. Ditto Edward Fox and Keith Barron. And then there was Leslie Phillips, whom I took back for a second time, despite the fact that the first time he left me was because I sent him a script that he thought was way below his bottom line in terms of quality. He subsequently accepted the job, did his own deal and avoided paying my very modest 10 per cent commission.

In those days, 10 per cent was very much the going rate; now agents take anything between 12.5 and 15 per cent, with a few having a laugh and charging as much as 20 per cent – though not to David Tomlinson of *Mary Poppins* fame, who didn't pay commission to agents at all, because he thought that having him on their books was reward enough. Nobody had a higher opinion of David Tomlinson than he did of himself. Although he was a charming and witty man, and extremely good company, I didn't think I wanted to represent him 'gratis', so I passed on his kind invitation.

Leslie's behaviour was fairly bad, but was it worse than that of David Hemmings, who I took back for a second innings, got a job and asked round for a drink the day before he started filming?

'I'm not drinking any more, so I'll just have a Coke,' he said as I was preparing the drinks.

'Actually, is that rum?' he went on. 'Sling in a measure, that won't count, it's barely alcoholic.'

Several 'barely alcoholic' rums later, he weaved his way home.

The following morning I had a call from his producer.

'Do you know what time David is proposing to turn up this morning for filming?' he asked.

'Well, whatever his call time is, I guess.'

'That was three hours ago, and he is not answering his phone or his doorbell and the car we sent for him is still waiting outside his house,' he snapped. A full-time US resident at the time, David had rented a small flat in Fulham while he filmed the television series.

'Let me see if I can get hold of his wife,' I said.

'David?' came the reply from the then Mrs Hemmings, whom I had woken up in LA. 'He's in Paris. He arrived there this morning.'

'He's meant to be on a location in London,' I said as calmly as I could.

'I don't know about that. He told me he was going to Paris today, weeks ago. I think you must be a bit confused, Michael.'

There was clearly no point in further discussion with her. David, as per usual, was going to do exactly what David wanted to do, and to hell with anyone else. To say that the producer was furious was an understatement, and of course he blamed me entirely for not being able to control my clients. He also accused me of being wholly unprofessional, unscrupulous and immoral, and moving him on to a more lucrative job in a movie.

'Don't be ridiculous. It was me that talked him into doing this job in the first place. He felt that it was way below his pay grade. To be honest, David has taken us both for a ride, and he will definitely be looking for new representation.'

'Great, where does that leave me? A drama series with no leading man, a schedule that's shot to bits and a crew standing around doing nothing. When an agent tells me that we have a deal, I assume that we have. I can't believe that you have done this to me. I will *never* trust you again, and certainly never use another client of yours in the future, Michael.'

The producer was a top-league player at the BBC. I couldn't leave things here.

'I think I might be able to help you with a re-cast.'

'Fuck off, Michael! I've just told you—'

'What about Edward Fox?' I cut in. 'He's *very* reliable. I've just taken him back for a second time.'

'He's too short,' the producer shouted.

'Nonsense, he's a perfect height and he could start tomorrow.' He hung up.

Martin Shaw played the part.

I was very lucky to have some really good clients, although one or two of the 'I-know-the-face-but-not-the-name' actors, who I took on mainly because they were nice people and assured me that they would be no trouble, turned out to be anything but. One such was an actor who had been a bit of a TV name in his youth, but who had had a quietish time of late. He took me to The Garrick Club, where we were both members, and bought me a very good lunch. One of the club's rules states that members must not use any part of the club premises for business purposes. Well, my host talked of nothing else but business for the entire hour and a half we were together, and then only of his business. He was clearly very unhappy with his current agent, who he thought took him for granted, and was thinking of giving the whole thing up. He had a very rich wife and I wanted to tell him that I thought giving it up would be a really good idea.

Very few actors work all the time. It has become an incredibly overcrowded industry. When I first started as an agent, *Spotlight*, the casting directory, consisted of one large volume for actors and a much slimmer one for actresses. Today there are eight volumes for each and, although there are now literally hundreds of TV channels, they are awash with reality and quiz shows, property makeover programmes and cookery shows, so work for actors has not increased in real terms. Quite simply, there are just too many people who call themselves 'actors'; there are even stand-up comedians who think they're actors nowadays. So agents have to be even more ruthless than ever about who they take on.

But *I'm-thinking-of-giving-it-all-up* was sure there must be the occasional film or television part that would be right for him – after all, he had been a marquee name once (albeit on relatively small marquees), and that must count for something? It was at this point that I made a fatal mistake. I tend not to drink much at lunchtime, perhaps a glass of white wine, but as it had been an exhausting encounter, I accepted his invitation to join him in a glass of club port.

As I emptied my second glass, he reassured me that he wouldn't be any trouble and would certainly not pester me with phone calls. But if anything came up, he'd be very grateful if I would mention him. And he quite understood that I had much bigger fish to fry. Indeed, he didn't need me to suggest him for jobs, just to keep an eye out for him. None of this was logical in any way, but I succumbed: the club port had done its job for him. Two days later he rang me.

'Is anything happening?'

This was to be a daily occurrence from then on.

He left me a couple of months later and went back to his previous agent.

The letter of departure is a work of art, and I have on occasion helped new clients write theirs. It's best to do it by letter. I suppose it would be reasonable via email these days – although to my old-fashioned mind not appropriate – but by text is totally unacceptable. The *Dear John* letter should be along these lines:

Dear Agent,

This is a very difficult letter for me to write [*which is why I have got my new agent to write it for me*] particularly in light of the close and fruitful relationship we have enjoyed over the past years [*although a lot less close since it became a lot less fruitful*]. Please be assured that I have not come to this decision without giving it a great deal of thought [*and after approaching several other agents and finding one that wants to take me on*]. But I feel like a rudderless ship [*I thought you would appreciate a nautical analogy as you spend most weekends – starting on Thursday evening and ending on Monday morning – on that bloody boat in the Solent*] and have decided very reluctantly [*eagerly*], to make a change in my representation [*sack you*].

I know this letter will come as a shock to you [*because I've been too much of a coward to give you any clues as to how pissed off I am with you*], but I thought it best to write and avoid the unnecessary embarrassment that a meeting in your office or over lunch would cause us both [*and I was worried that you might talk me into staying with you*].

I would, however, like to thank you for all you have done for me over the years [*although to be honest, most of the jobs you claimed to have got me, I got myself*], and I sincerely hope that we will remain close friends in the future [*if I ever see you again it will be too soon*].

Love,

Judas

Agents are very good at talking you into doing things you don't want to do; that's probably why you went to them in the first place, for their skill in talking producers and casting directors into casting *you* when they really wanted someone else. The office meeting is a definite no-go area: the agent in all probability will guess why you're coming to see them and the atmosphere will be tense and the meeting short; full of recriminations, accusations of ingratitude and hurt. Agents can be sensitive souls, especially when they are losing a big chunk of income.

Unless of course it's the agent who wants *you* to leave. I represented a few actors who I couldn't wait to see the back of; people who were never off the phone asking 'Is anything happening?' Not to you it isn't, I always longed to say, but never did.

Elaine Stritch sacked me after she went back to America but forgot to tell me, and I did find it a little upsetting when she took the job that I had suggested her for but through another agent. The only upside was that the producer told me I would have got a much better deal for her than the new agent did.

I also had a long list of 'Ones Who Got Away', actors and actresses who I desperately wanted to represent but never did. I couldn't understand how they could conceivably prefer being with that charmless, common agent they went to instead of me. And, even worse, when they left them and went on to even more rank, talentless, agents, instead of returning to me.

And of course I made many mistakes along the way, including telling a sixteen-year-old Robert Pattinson that there were already too many pretty young actors in the business; he was too tall and he should stick to modelling. I was too star struck to throw my hat into the ring when Anthony Hopkins was looking for an agent. I had always been a huge admirer of Tony's work. He's not a man to remain in character during the shooting of a film, as do some others I could name. *Shadowlands* and *Remains of the Day* are two of my all time favourite films. I was lucky enough to visit the set of the latter, when my client James Fox was filming with Tony and Emma Thompson, on location in Gloucestershire. I found myself next to Tony in the queue for lunch and we chatted for ten minutes, whilst waiting to be served.

Afterwards I went on to the set where the director James Ivory was rehearsing a key scene, involving Tony's character, the butler Stevens, and his elderly father played by Peter Vaughan. Whilst they were lighting the scene, Tony was pacing up and down, running over his lines and psyching himself up for the big scene, and as he walked past me to begin his final rehearsal, he gave me a beaming smile and said: 'Nice lunch?'

Julian Fellowes, creator of *Downton Abbey*, claimed to have written to me asking about representation and told me that I had written back turning him down, as he would clash with Nigel Havers and Ian Ogilvy. This suggestion I vehemently denied, until I went to stay with him in his house in Dorset and he produced my letter. I said that it was a forgery, or possibly written without my knowledge by an overzealous secretary, but he didn't buy that, on account of my recognisable italic handwriting, knocked into me by the Benedictine monks. I advised a young Chiwetel Ejiofor, while he was at the National Youth Theatre in *Othello*, that he would get absolutely nowhere with that name and he should definitely change it. I didn't spot the talent of Damian Lewis at the Regent's Park Open Air Theatre, and I mistimed my approach to a young blade playing the juvenile lead in a play at the National Theatre with my client Richard Pasco, who suggested I write to him, as he was looking to find his first agent. Sadly Ralph Fiennes had just gone elsewhere.

Timing is all in this business. Though I did at least get it right a few times. I helped snap up Colin Firth and Michael Fassbender at the Drama Centre, and Daniel Day-Lewis at the Bristol Old Vic. Of course, there were dozens of actors who I also took on and looked after of whom nobody has ever heard, then or since, but – as with many other businesses – it's only the successful ones that count.

Ultimately, I found the job of being an agent frustrating, as I had no real creative involvement, other than reading scripts. Once the deal is done, the agent's role peters out. So Nigel Havers and I decided to form a production company, which we called – with huge originality – Havahall. It was formed after the 1990 Broadcasting Act had deregulated the television industry, requiring 25 per cent of the networks' output to come from independent production companies. I soon discovered, however, that production could be just as frustrating as being an agent – probably more so.

3

At Home with the Parents

Beckenham in Kent. That's what sold it to my mother. I was about to go away to boarding school, and Nora thought that having parents living in Kent was more '*à la carte*' – Nora's phrase for describing the social class that she aspired to be part of – than living in Penge. Penge, SE20 may have been only a mile away from Beckenham, but class-wise it was a world away; even more so when she found out that it had been the home of Thomas Crapper, the inventor of the modern-day flush toilet.

When they bought 43 Foxgrove Avenue in 1950 – on a crescent of 1920s detached, suburban villas – Nora tried to get rid of the numbers.

'Why don't we call it The Pines?' she asked my father, Jack.

True, there were two pine trees in the back garden, but as the run of houses in the crescent went consecutively 41, 42, 43, 44, it would have been a little strange to stick 'The Pines' in between numbers 42 and 44. Moreover, the postman, whom Nora didn't like because he was far too familiar and called her Nora once when he came round for his Christmas box, said that the Post Office wouldn't agree to it. Anyway, my father Jack thought it was a bad idea and that was the end of it.

43 Foxgrove Avenue was a classic suburban house in the 'Tudorbethan' style. Nora used to call it 'Arts and Crafts' to her friends at the Bromley School of Art, but that was one of Nora's many fantasies. We had a breakfast room, where we never had breakfast; we had breakfast in the kitchen. We had a dining room where we never dined; we dined in the breakfast room. The dining room was seldom used; only for Christmas and the very rare occasions when people came to dinner. We had a lounge but were never allowed to call it the lounge because that was very common, another favourite word of Nora's, the opposite to *à la carte*. It had to be called the drawing room, which was another misnomer. (The dictionary definition of a drawing room is 'a room in a large private house in which guests can be received and entertained.') I suppose it could have been worse; she could have called it the morning room, thereby joining the other incorrectly named rooms in the house, as a room that was never used in the mornings.

The drawing room housed our small black-and-white television set, which bore no relation to the enormous sets of today. In spite of its modest size, Nora considered a visible television set, when not in use, to be beyond the pale. So she had it covered in a thick green velvet cloth and placed on a tea trolley, so that it could be pushed out of sight into the corner of the lounge (sorry, drawing room). There was also a 'toilet', a word that was, of course, as welcome as an outbreak of dysentery, which had to be called 'the lavatory' at all times. And the seat had to be put down after flushing, a vain hope of Nora's, given that she shared the house with three men. As with the television set, the loo roll had to be hidden, in this case under the skirts of a knitted doll, to save anyone from the embarrassment of having to look at it. There were moments in my childhood when I thought that if my mother could have knitted a cover to shroud my father with, she would have done.

In the garden, apart from the pine trees, there was a small crazy-paved patio, with a couple of worn-out teak chairs, which Nora referred to as 'the terrace'. 'Come and sit on the terrace,' she'd announce grandly, on the very rare occasions that the neighbours – the Millers at No. 42 and the Mellors at No. 44 – managed to get over the threshold. We only had two garden chairs, so Jack had to bring out the mahogany dining-room chairs, which were extremely uncomfortable and certainly not conducive to lounging out on 'the terrace'. The only other feature of our classic suburban garden was a structure, which Jack referred to as the shed (because that's what it was), but Nora called the gazebo, on account of it having two small windows.

Nora Whitehall had a very vivid imagination, which is perhaps why she was such a talented artist, but had far too many of what used to be referred to as 'airs and graces'. One had to admire her aspirational drive, although it often got out of control. I remember one weekend when Nora got carried away while we were sitting on the terrace and suggested to my cousin Jennifer that we all had tea in the gazebo. She was not pleased when Jack reminded her that the 'gazebo' not only contained some garden tools, a wheelbarrow and a lawn mower, but also two bags of manure. I often thought that in another life she could have made a wonderful estate agent, with her gift for exaggeration and embellishment when describing things.

One of my parents' few friends was a man called Gerard Usher-Smith. Gerard was a devout Catholic, an old boy of Ampleforth, a prominent member of the Catholic church in Beckenham and, as I found out to my cost some years later, an ardent follower of the renowned swindler Charles Ponzi.

Gerard was an insurance broker by trade, and also looked after my parents' modest financial affairs. Jack was never a big fan of his and wasn't sure whether Nora's trust in Gerard was solely because he was

Catholic and went to church every Sunday, which of course didn't mean he was either good with money or honest with it. In Gerard's case, he turned out to be neither.

When in 1969, I was in my late twenties, he heard from Nora that I'd inherited some money from my grandfather, and offered to invest it for me. I would provide finance for one of his trusted clients (also a Catholic) by way of a private mortgage on his house – all completely risk-free, of course – and I would get a much higher rate of interest from him than I could possibly get elsewhere. The agreement that Gerard had drawn up for me looked fine – these were the bad old days of unregulated financial advisors – so I handed over my five thousand pounds (£90,000 in today's money) and waited for the interest to roll in. I had, of course, already taken some advice from my brother.

'I'd tell him to fuck off,' said Barry sagely.

'He told me he was doing some financial work for the monks at Ampleforth,' said Nora. 'They certainly wouldn't be involved with someone who wasn't completely honest.'

In any case, the interest cheques came in at the end of each month and I had the security of a mortgage on a nice detached house in Banstead, owned by a Major Pritchard. But then, quite suddenly, as know-all Barry had predicted, the cheques stopped coming. I rang

Gerard, who assured me everything was fine. A month passed, still no cheque. I had a few more conversations with him, and then he became aggressive.

'I've told you already, you'll get your money. This is a very good investment I've put your way, Michael, so don't be greedy,' he ranted at me down the phone.

A few weeks later, I plucked up the courage to call him again. The phone had been disconnected. Saint Gerard had done a runner.

'I did warn you,' Barry said helpfully. 'The guy's a crook. I'm amazed you didn't see it coming.'

A week later, I received a letter from Major Pritchard telling me that he had a mortgage on my house and was going to have to call in the money, as he had had no interest payments from me. Moreover, his mortgage broker had disappeared. The major reacted very badly to the news that I had the identical arrangement on his house, and that my mortgage broker had disappeared too. We met up and discovered that our so-called mortgages were valueless and that our broker, Mr Usher-Smith, had effectively stolen our money. It turned out that he'd pulled the same trick on dozens of other gullible investors; many of them retired army officers who had handed over their pensions to him for safekeeping. (Charles Ponzi would have been proud of him.) The police eventually caught up with Gerard and he did a couple of years in an open prison in Arundel. I had a plan to round up all the ex-soldiers he had conned and head down to Arundel to sort him out, but Major Pritchard advised against it: most of those he had swindled were now in their early seventies.

I did however, manage to track Gerard down after his release and sent him an abusive letter. Nora was shocked that I'd been so rude to him. She had heard – she never divulged from whom – that his wife was seriously ill and he'd needed the money to pay her medical bills. I subsequently received a letter from his solicitors accusing me of harassment, which I thought was ridiculous. I had only said that I would kill him if I didn't get my £5,000 back. Neither happened.

'You should have told him to fuck off in the first place,' said Barry.

Oh, the joys of 1950s Beckenham. The Odeon cinema was a favourite, where my mother and father took me to see films that they loved, like *The Lavender Hill Mob* and *The Ladykillers*. We also used to go to the Penge Empire – my mother didn't mind visiting Penge; she just didn't want to live there – where they had a weekly repertory company, led at one time by the then unknown Arthur Lowe, later to become Captain Mainwaring in *Dad's Army*. Lunches for the discerning crowd were taken at The Whim on Beckenham High Street, an establishment run by two middle-aged ladies. It was a favourite of Nora's, who greatly admired the owners, who produced homemade food from a tiny kitchen in the back and lived above the shop.

Barry said that they were lesbians, which made Nora very cross as they were Catholic and took the plate round at St Edmund's Church on Sundays.

'They might still be lesbians,' said Barry.

'What do lesbians actually do?' I asked fifteen-year-old Barry. (I was twelve.)

'I can't remember . . . I don't think it's anything very interesting.'

One day we decided to get a dog. Jack was all for it, Nora firmly against. However, if Jack agreed to buy a *pedigree* dog, her mind might be changed. Something small and elegant, perhaps a Pekingese like that nice '*à la carte*' lady who lived in The Avenue. A smarter address than ours, with older Victorian houses that had larger gardens, The Avenue was sadly out of Jack and Nora's price range. Nora tracked down Mrs Crichton-Stuart and cold-called her for a chat about Pekingeses. She returned home, armed with the name of the breeder and, before you could shout 'walkies', we had a fully registered and Kennel Club-approved Pekingese dog. Nora decided to call him Foxgrove Candy Floss.

For almost his entire time with us, Candy Floss was in a very bad mood. Perhaps this was because of his name.

Nora had intended to call him Foxgrove, but the distinctly feminine 'Candy Floss' had stuck, certainly with us boys, much to Nora's chagrin; she resolutely stuck to Foxgrove. He presented his sulky demeanour by biting anyone who approached him, particularly if the person was anywhere in the vicinity of his food. The bite was usually preceded by a growl (upper lip quivering before a full baring of teeth), which Barry and I referred to as the 'frisks'. The next stage was the full bite, which we called 'the snaps'.

'Candy Floss is very snappy this evening,' Jack would say when he got back from work, with the dog's jaws clamped to the turn-ups of his suit trousers. 'Should I take him for a walk?' Walking Candy Floss was a nightmare, and Jack was the only member of the family who attempted it.

One Saturday afternoon Father O'Malley, the local Catholic priest to whom Nora had been sucking up for years, had finally accepted an invitation to tea, but made the fatal error of putting his outstretched hand into Candy Floss's basket to give him a pat. Unfortunately, he failed to notice that Candy Floss was enjoying a piece of leftover scone retrieved from the floor. He bit Father O'Malley so severely and gave him such a fright that he had to lie down on the spare bed for an hour; once, of course, we had prised Candy's jaws open and Nora had bandaged up his hand. In spite of all her best efforts, she never managed to get Father O'Malley to accept an invitation to 43 Foxgrove Avenue again, nor was she offered a return visit to the presbytery. And she never let him hear her confession again, in case he recognised her voice.

When I was at school I could never take confession seriously enough. As a Catholic I was supposed to believe that the monk who might just have been teaching me French in a classroom, or the monk who had recently given me a detention for fooling around in prep and who was now hearing my confession, was not in fact Father Wilfred or Father Stephen, he was *in persona Christi*, acting as Jesus and God. Now that was all very well, but I couldn't make that leap of faith, so I always disguised my voice in the confessional, in case the monk hearing my confession recognised it; or, if I was convinced he had, I would always edit my list of sins, confessing lies, selfishness and jealousy, but avoiding all mention of cheating, impure thoughts and, worst of all, masturbation. At one stage in my school life, there was an elderly monk called Father Gregory. When it was time for confessions (once a week was the norm), his confessional would always have a long snaking queue outside it, while the other five would have one or two boys waiting outside. And why? Father Gregory wore two heavy-duty hearing aids but was still as deaf as a post. Forgiveness from him was a given for all those who hadn't bought into the *in persona Christi* theory.

Back in Foxgrove Avenue, following several other unprovoked attacks over the years, Uncle Peter tried to lift Candy Floss out of his basket after a particularly boozy Christmas lunch and was bitten on the nose in return for his show of seasonal affection. This was the last straw: Candy Floss had to be returned to the breeder for rehoming. The breeder suggested rather grandly that the cause of the dog's feral behaviour was the modest size of our garden. If only we had lived in The Avenue and had had a garden the size of Mrs Crichton-Stuart's.

Appearance was everything in Nora's world. She had always been interested in art and music but, as with so many of her interests, they were skin deep and only really served the purpose of covering up her massive inferiority complex and providing her with some much-needed gravitas.

We had a piano in our 'lounge', which Nora would play from time to time, despite her very limited repertoire. She played Rachmaninoff's Piano Concerto No. 2, but only the opening chords. She would then move into a piece of her own composition, which was a variation on Rachmaninoff's work, but considerably easier to play. She also entertained us with the first eight bars of

Beethoven's Moonlight Sonata, cutting to the chase with the last six bars of the piece, the whole performance taking less than a minute, as opposed to the more conventional fifteen. She was a fan of Liberace and hugely admired his playing of the classics, similarly improvised, or the one hundred and fifty-three pages of Tchaikovsky's Piano Concerto No. 1, of which he only performed the first twelve and the last four, adding four of his own in the middle.

A shopping trip with my mother to the West End was always an event of Lord Mayor's Show proportions. Smart dress code was *de rigueur*. Even if we were going to Gorringes in Victoria to buy new school shoes, Nora would go to the hairdresser in Beckenham High Street beforehand, for a rinse and blow-dry, and take whatever outfit she was planning to wear on the trip, for a freshen-up at Sketchley next door.

When my father was working in the fur department at Gorringes, he was allowed a discount on anything bought in the store. But Nora never took advantage of the discount: admitting to a shop assistant that her husband actually worked there would have been anathema to her. Of course, she never went near the fur department, as meeting Jack on the shop floor would have sent her into major trauma. She would, however, wander into some of the other departments – ladies' woollens was always a favourite.

'Could you show me this in a bottle green,' she'd ask. 'Or taupe?' I have never got to grips with what colour that actually is, but it sounds horrible.

Seeing as she was always deeply embarrassed at the size of her substantial bust, she never tried on anything in the shop; the garments were merely held up in front of her by the assistant, as they both peered into the mirror. I would stand silently beside her, feigning interest.

Lunch was usually taken at the Kardomah, not a particularly exciting venue for a schoolboy on his holidays, but Nora liked it because it wasn't expensive and the customers always looked quite '*à la carte*', as indeed did the food. 'You always get a nice crowd at the Kardomah,' she'd say, not that she would have dreamt of speaking to anyone there. Jack preferred the Salad Bowl at Lyons Corner House, which he thought less stuffy. But it dropped off Nora's list when she found herself standing next to the saleswoman from Sketchley in Beckenham, shovelling potato salad on to her plate.

'That blouse came up nicely, didn't it Mrs Whitehall?' she said.

Nora went right off her lunch.

'Lyons can be very common at lunchtime,' she told me later. 'Let's stick to the Kardomah.'

Of course I much preferred the Salad Bowl, as I could pile my plate full of 'common' things like tinned sweetcorn, Russian salad and luncheon meat. The Kardomah was all Welsh rarebits and mushroom omelettes.

I remember the day my mother telephoned Gibney's, the butchers in the High Street, and asked them to put aside some steak and kidney for a pie she was planning to bake, for a rare visit from my Uncle Cyril and Auntie Alice.

'And I don't want no kidney, which is what you gave me last time,' she told Mr Gibney firmly. 'And make sure the steak is tender.'

'So you don't want no kidney?' he repeated.

'Correct,' said Nora.

Jack picked the meat up on his way home from Gorringes, and when Nora opened up the package, it was all steak. She rang Mr Gibney in a fury.

'Where is my kidney?' she demanded.

'But Mrs Whitehall, you said you didn't want no kidney.'

Entertaining at 43 Foxgrove Avenue was a rare event. Jack would have liked a wife who helped him a bit on the business front, but as working in the fur department at Gorringes wasn't what Nora had ever wanted for Jack, help and support tended to be in short supply. There was, however, one occasion when Jack invited the fur buyer at Gorringes, and therefore Jack's immediate boss, to supper. Miss Short was an elegant but rather humourless woman in her late forties, who Barry thought was probably lesbian; indeed he seemed to think that any unmarried woman over twenty-five years of age was that way inclined. As I still didn't know what a lesbian was, I couldn't really broach the subject with anyone other than Barry, so I had to take his judgements on trust. Nora had, of course, gone to a lot of trouble to ensure that Miss Short had a good time, though that was something she looked as though she had never had in her life.

'Where are the place cards?' Nora asked Jack, as she was putting the final touches to the dining-room table.

'But there are only four of us,' said Jack. 'Barry is going out and Miss Short's friend has got flu.'

Miss Short's friend seemed to have flu on a round-the-clock basis. In fact nobody had ever met Miss Short's friend, and there was a suspicion that he might not even exist.

'Or be a woman, more likely,' Barry said.

'I still think we should have place cards,' said Nora. 'Michael can do them in his nice italic writing ... put the drinks out on the sideboard ... and make sure you offer the dry sherry, Jack. I'm sure Miss Short doesn't drink sweet sherry.'

Although she thought it was very common, Nora loved sweet sherry and loathed dry sherry, but when anyone came round for a drink, anything sweet was hidden from view and Nora put on a pretence of enjoying Tío Pepe.

The evening was eventful in that it resulted in Nora having one of her 'states'.

'Your mother is in one of her *states*,' Jack would tell Barry and me. 'Go and talk to her.'

'No chance!' said Barry. 'She's not going to listen to me!'

So it was left to me to go upstairs to her bedroom where she was packing.

'I'm off,' she'd announce. 'I'm going up to London.'

She'd stomp down the stairs, slam the front door and head for Beckenham Junction to catch the 'all-stations' train from Orpington to Victoria. Jack and Barry would wheel the television out of the corner of the lounge and start watching it (Nora would normally make her exit just after supper). I would be worried that I'd never see her again and would run off to get her before she reached the station. She never walked very quickly, hoping that one of us would catch her up and bring her home. It was always me. There would occasionally be tears, and she'd always accuse Jack of not appreciating her.

'You never take me out for dinner, or the theatre. We never go on holiday. And why don't you ever bring home something like a couple of tickets for the opera?' she'd wail.

'You don't even like opera,' Jack would protest. 'You always tell me to turn off that screaming woman when there's opera on the radio.'

'That's not the point. It's the thought that counts.'

After a few more tears and a hug, she'd go to bed and it would never be mentioned again ... until she had another 'state'.

The dinner party started well enough. Nora served her signature dish of melon with a glacé cherry on top, overcooked roast lamb (Nora was a genius at overcooking meat) and sherry trifle, washed down with a bottle of Blue Nun served at room temperature. Jack would probably lower the tone by drinking light ale. Over the coffee, Miss Short asked Nora if she ever went to the theatre.

'Nora doesn't really like the theatre,' replied Jack before Nora had a chance to speak. 'But we do go to the pictures quite a lot, don't we dear?'

'I wouldn't say I don't *like* the theatre,' said Nora sharply. 'You never ask me to go to the theatre.'

'Jack and I went once, didn't we,' said Miss Short. 'To a matinee of *Spider's Web*.'

Jack looked embarrassed.

'With Margaret Lockwood,' Miss Short carried on. 'It was an Agatha Christie. Although not as good as *The Mousetrap*.'

'You don't even like murder mysteries,' snapped Nora.

'Please may I get down?' I asked. 'I need to sort out some stuff in my room.' I sensed that we might be moving towards a murder mystery of our own.

The rest of the evening – certainly from where I was watching it at the top of the stairs – was tense. Nora went into a sulk, and Jack and Miss Short started talking shop.

'I nearly sold one of those Persian lamb coats this morning,' said Jack. 'The lady said she'd talk to her husband and come back to me tomorrow.'

'Yes, they're nice quality those coats,' said Miss Short. 'I'm glad people are wearing Persian lamb again.'

Nora clearly didn't wish to join in this conversation – Jack had never given her a Persian lamb coat – and swept up the plates. Her eyes were now bulging and she had gritted teeth, very reminiscent of Candy Floss when he was transitioning from 'the frisks' to 'the snaps'. Miss Short took this as a sign that the party was over.

As Miss Short's car headed off down Foxgrove Avenue, Nora exploded.

'So you've been having cosy afternoons at the theatre with Miss Short, eh? You never ask me to go to the theatre with you,' said Nora.

(I was still sitting at the top of the stairs, listening to this scenario playing out. I'd been here often before.)

'You never want to go to the theatre,' said Jack. 'The last time I suggested we go, you said that I should go on my own.'

'That was because you wanted to take me to the Penge Empire to see that ghastly variety show with Tommy Trinder and David Whitfield. You've never suggested a West End matinee of a Margaret Lockwood play, and you know how much I like her. I can't believe you went to see her with that woman!'

Nora was winding herself up into a state.

'You shower that Short woman with tickets but not your wife!'

'Actually the tickets were free,' said Jack.

'Oh, I see, free tickets as well. You never get free tickets for me!'

'I didn't get the tickets – Mary did.'

'Oh, *Mary* is it?'

Jack carried on tightening the noose round his own neck, while I sat tensely on the laundry basket, fearing the worst.

'She served this very nice lady who bought a musquash coat, which she wanted altered,' said Jack. 'And she was so pleased with the alterations, she gave Mary two tickets for the play.'

'Who was this woman?' asked Nora.

'The producer's wife, I think.'

'Well presumably she'll be asking you out next, and then you'll have two women on the go . . . excluding me, of course. I've had enough of this. I'm off.' Nora then swept across the sitting room, up the stairs, passing me hiding behind the laundry basket, and into her bedroom, slamming the door behind her.

I tiptoed downstairs and helped Jack with the washing up.

'Aren't you going up to talk to her?' I asked. 'She seems in quite a state.'

'No, she'll be fine. You know your mother, she likes to get herself in a state.'

The front door opened. It was Barry back from an evening with his friend Larry.

'How was the lezzie?' he said.

'Don't be rude about Miss Short,' replied Jack. 'And she isn't a lesbian. In fact your mother seems to think I'm having an affair with her.'

'What's an affair?' I asked, having come out from behind the laundry basket.

Barry laughed. Although deeply upset by the developments, I mistakenly thought this was my moment to address the lesbian question.

'Can I ask you something, Daddy?'

'Yes, of course dear,' he said sympathetically, sensing my distress.

'What exactly do lesbians do?'

Before Jack had a chance to reply, the bedroom door was flung open, and Nora – in suede hat, coat, gloves and scarf – came thumping down the stairs, dragging a huge brown suitcase behind her.

'All I've ever wanted is one attic room, an easel and my paints,' she said breathlessly. 'I'll let you all know where I'm going to be living in future.'

Then the door slammed behind her.

'Isn't anyone going after her?' I asked.

'No point,' said Barry casually. 'She'll be back. You know Mother. I'm for bed.'

'But she looked really upset,' I said.

'I think it's time you went to bed too, Michael,' said Jack. 'I'll wait up for her.'

I lay in bed, wide awake, waiting for her return. Would she ever come back? I was only twelve, for God's sake, and needed a mother. Sure enough, half an hour later, I heard the key in the door and Nora slamming it behind her.

The following morning she told me that she had missed the last train to Victoria and the suitcase was too heavy to carry back, so she'd left it in the stationmaster's office. He'd been extremely helpful and very charming. Jack, who was nursing a stiff neck, having been banished to the gazebo for the night, as a result of the revelations of his outings with Miss Short, resisted the temptation of suggesting that Nora might like to go to the theatre with him one evening.

'What do lesbians actually do?' I asked Barry later.

'I'm not sure exactly,' he replied, 'but it's definitely very weird and I think needs special equipment. Shall we ask Miss Short next time she comes to supper?'

'I don't think there'll be a next time,' I replied, and I was right.

4

The Pr*ducers

In *Adventures in the Screen Trade*, William Goldman tells the following tale.

'I was at a gathering once where a star was chatting socially with an agent not his own. And the star was being funny and charming and we all listened and laughed and then the star began to tell a story that had happened that day, on a taxi ride in from the airport, and the agent said, quietly but with amazement, "You mean they didn't send a limo?" The star shrugged and said he didn't want one and went on with his taxi ride material. But I was watching and I saw the look that passed ever so briefly when the agent cut in with the limo line. It did not surprise me when I learned shortly afterwards that the star had changed agencies ...'

I wonder how long the star stayed with his new agent? Probably not long. As the maxim goes, usually credited to Ian McKellen, 'Changing agents is like changing deck-chairs on the *Titanic*.'

I was now representing quite an elegant stable of thoroughbred actors, but the *Titanic* analogy was beginning to haunt me. What if they all left and moved to other deckchairs? Could Havahall be the way forward? No other agents had gone into production; could I lead the way?

Nigel Havers was riding high, having just made *The Charmer* for ITV, a role that was to follow him throughout his career. 'TV Charmer Dumps Missus' was one of the *Sun*'s classier headlines when they reported Nigel's impending divorce from his first wife Caro.

The Long-Haired Boy, a novel by Christopher Matthew published in the 1980s, was inspired by the life of Richard Hillary. Hillary had been an RAF pilot, who had been badly burnt when his Spitfire was shot down during the Battle of Britain, and subsequently became one of pioneering plastic surgeon Archibald McIndoe's guinea pigs at his hospital in East Grinstead. In 1990, with the help of the screenwriter Allan Prior, we put together an outline for a six-part serial loosely based on Hillary's story, which we called *A Perfect Hero*, and sent it over to LWT's Head of Drama, Nick Elliott.

We waited. And waited. And waited.

And then one Friday afternoon a letter arrived by hand. 'Liked the idea initially but . . .' followed by a lot of reasons why Nick was turning down the project. It was 'too old-fashioned ... too elitist ... too

downbeat . . . felt derivative of other dramas . . . predictable . . . would not work as a returning series . . . absence
of feel-good factor . . . not commissioning any medical
shows at the moment . . . wartime drama too depressing
for weekends . . . lacking humour . . .'

Nick was never one to mince his words, no sweet-
ening of the pill for him. If he didn't like something,
you got a straight 'no' without any trimmings. No
sorrys, no regrets, no highlighting the many plus
sides of the idea, and certainly no hopes that we
would be working together on something else in the
future.

Lacking humour? How could we possibly have
presented a humorous project to Nick about a young
pilot who is horrifically burnt, his face and body disfig-
ured beyond recognition, his spirit broken and his life in
ruins, and who is then subjected to years of painful
surgery, as full of laughs? How many jokes can you
make about burnt pilots?

Nigel and I were deeply depressed. This was our first
foray into television production and it looked as though
it might well be our last.

'Perhaps we should re-present it as a comedy?' said
Allan Prior. 'Like *MASH* but centred more on innovative
plastic surgery during the Second World War.'

For a moment I thought that it might work, and then
I realised he was joking.

The word 'predictable' had been the most hurtful remark for me.

Of course if you are trapped in a burning plane and end up looking like Frankenstein's monster, you're going to be pretty pissed off. But if ultimately you find the courage to face the future, is that 'predictable'?

Anyway, we decided that there was no point in getting bitter about it, which of course we all did. And then on Monday morning another letter arrived from Nick.

The race meeting he'd been going to on the Saturday had been called off, so he'd had a bit of time on his hands and had had another look at our outline. People want to watch drama with a bit of substance at the weekends, not just endless rehashes of the same thing. *A Perfect Hero* (he loved the title) was an uplifting story set in a fascinating period of history. Heroic, original and laced with subtle humour, it wouldn't work as a returning series but that wasn't what we were pitching – it would be perfect as a six-part serial. And what he particularly liked was its 'unpredictability'.

Nick had always carried the tag that once he made up his mind, no power on earth would prevent him from changing it. Many an idea he 'loved' over lunch at The Ivy he hated the following morning, but this was the other way round. We were ecstatic.

A few months later the director James Cellan Jones came on board. Cellan Jones treated me, a first-time producer, with derision, and although I had developed the project and cast the two leads (James Fox was to play the surgeon), he made it very clear that *he* was in charge. I attempted to get Hilary the extremely small part of an RAF driver, a piece of minor casting that would normally have been nodded through by a casting director. But no, Cellan Jones would have to interview Hilary, along with several other actresses, and predictably decided she wasn't 'right' for the part. In fact the girl he cast was the same age as Hilary and was different from her in only one respect – she couldn't drive. This meant that we had to find and then employ a driving double for her. To save money, the crew often pushed the car while she mimed driving it.

Towards the end of the shoot, I had a call from Nick Elliott to say that he had just had an irate and extremely rude Cellan Jones on the phone. He wanted to cut a long and rather pointless scene in one of the episodes and Cellan Jones was refusing to allow him to do so.

'I told Cellan Jones that I had final say on this and that we didn't need the scene, and anyway it wasn't any good even if we had,' said Nick. 'Cellan Jones then started shouting and accusing me of butchering his film. Butchering his bloody film? It was a scene featuring two actors whom we'd never seen before, and would never see again, playing cards in gas masks.'

'I remember that scene, Nick. It never worked,' I

replied supportively. He was, after all, Head of Drama.

'And then,' continued Nick, 'he started bellowing at me and then ...' he paused for breath, 'and then, he called me a c**t!'

'I'm really sorry Nick,' I said, 'but I wouldn't get too upset about it. You know what he's like – and he is Welsh.'

'But he called me a c**t, Michael,' said Nick. 'Nobody's ever called me a c**t – well, not to my face anyway!'

I certainly knew several people who might have agreed with Cellan Jones's sentiments, but none who would have gone for the direct approach. He and Nick hardly spoke again. The launch party was a tense affair, but the series was well received and proved to be a successful start to my new career.

While I was working with LWT I had a meeting with Michael Grade, who was Controller of Programmes, to talk about Elaine Stritch, who had recently finished a successful series with Donald Sinden, *Two's Company*, which ran for four series from 1975 to 1979. LWT were looking for a new project for her. Michael was very charming, had a wonderful sense of humour and in those days didn't take life too seriously (he probably still doesn't). Having settled me down in his elegant office with a large gin and tonic he took a call on his internal phone.

'I'm really sorry, Michael, but I've got to see these two guys for a moment ... they were due here an hour ago. Would you mind sitting outside for a moment?'

As I walked out into the reception area, Michael followed me and ushered in the two people waiting outside.

'Michael, do you know Martin Shaw and Lewis Collins?'

In fact I didn't, although I knew who they were and that they were LWT's two glittering stars of *The Professionals*. They both looked very grumpy and were clearly not remotely interested in meeting me. They were there to ear-bash the other Michael, the important one. Before I'd had a chance to finish reading 'Saturday lunchtimes wouldn't be the same without *Saint and Greavsie*' in LWT's *What's New* magazine, they swept out of Michael's office, cutting me dead en route.

'God they're annoying,' said Michael as he replenished my drink, 'but *The Professionals* is a big show for us, so it's very important that we keep them happy.'

'Well, they certainly didn't look very happy to me,' I added helpfully.

'Why can't they be like Gordon Jackson, who is an absolute sweetheart?' wondered Michael.

'So what's the problem?'

'The problem is that neither of them wants to be doing *The Professionals*. Martin Shaw wants to be at the

National Theatre or the RSC and Lewis Collins wants to be in the SAS. Now let's talk about fun-loving, easy-going Elaine Stritch,' he said, lighting up a large Montecristo.

During my first few months as an agent in the late 60s, my boss Laurie Evans was summoned to Brighton to see a play, which his client Rex Harrison was touring in prior to opening in the West End. The play was called *The Lionel Touch* and had been written by a one-trick pony called George Hulme. Rex was attracted to the part of Lionel, a raffish, womanising artist, because the character was erratic and temperamental.

'A change of image for me, Laurie,' he told Evans. 'It will be quite a challenge for me.'

Laurie told me that he didn't think Rex playing someone erratic and temperamental would be much of a challenge.

Things were not going well in Brighton, with Rex threatening to leave the production on an almost daily basis. Laurie needed to protect his commission, Rex being one of the highest-paid actors in the business, so accompanied by his wife Mary and his very new assistant, me, we headed down to Brighton in his Rolls.

Mary was Laurie's second wife and was considerably younger than him. Tall, charming and attractive, she had been involved in the office management (some unfairly said catering) at MCA, the agency Laurie worked for before he set up London International with Robin Fox. Eyebrows were raised when Laurie and Mary got married, not just because she was marrying the boss, but also because of their considerable age difference.

As we settled down at a corner table at English's after the play, I sensed tension in the air.

'So, what did you think, Lol?' said Rex, sipping a glass of champagne. 'Did you like it?'

'Hugely, Rex,' replied Laurie. 'You have nothing whatsoever to worry about. We all thought you were magnificent . . .'

This took me slightly by surprise as, during the interval, which had gone on for ever due to a technical problem with the set, Laurie had said that it was the worst play he had ever seen and that Rex's performance was appalling. Rex had cut the play to shreds and removed all the serious stuff, which, in turn, had made Lionel more lovable. The play had been turned into a light comedy; the problem was that it wasn't funny.

'Did you miss the serious stuff, Lol?' asked Rex.

'Not a bit, Rex. Works much better without it,' lied Laurie.

I was beginning to get the hang of how this actor/agent thing worked.

'The man was a monster in the original script; not your kind of part at all, Rex.'

'So what about me then?' asked Rex, a question I was to be asked by clients many times in the future, and certainly one that Rex was not asking Laurie for the first time.

'What about you, Rex?' replied Laurie. 'You were, as I've already said, magnificent.'

Rex gave me a penetrating stare. I thought for a moment he was going to ask me what I thought of him, and I was trying to think of a word other than magnificent. 'Jolly good' flashed across my mind, but that would clearly have been inadequate. I was relieved to see Rex turn his head and direct his attentions to the young Mrs Evans. I had, after all, been warned in the car not to engage with Rex unless absolutely necessary; I also felt the pressure of Laurie's foot bearing down on my shoe.

Mary looked embarrassed. He was obviously waiting for her to speak, or was he?

'Was there nothing anyone didn't like?' he asked warmly.

Silence, and then . . .

'Well, to be honest Rex,' said Mary, 'and I probably don't know what I'm talking about, but I wonder whether at the end of Act One, it might possibly be better if you, well if you . . .'

'Shut up, you clockwork c**t,' shouted Rex. 'I'm not remotely interested in your opinions!'

At which point everyone leapt up from the table. A furious Laurie, a quivering Mary and a nervous me headed for the Rolls, as Rex stormed off up the street to his hotel.

By the time I arrived in the office the following morning, Laurie had sacked Rex on the phone and by letter, a first for him on both counts.

'How much does Rex earn a year,' I asked. 'Roughly?'

'Money has got nothing to do with it, Michael. How dare the c**t call my wife one . . . totally unacceptable. I wouldn't be Rex's agent if he was the last actor on earth. Now let's get on with some work.'

Rex and Laurie got back together six months later.

This emotive word caused more offence many years later when I was having dinner with Gyles Brandreth and his wife Michèle at their house in Barnes. The other guests, in addition to Hilary, were Neil and Christine Hamilton. Over dinner, the conversation got round to actors, and Gyles encouraged me to tell a story about Kenneth More that he'd heard many times before but seemed to enjoy. It did however require the use of the 'c' word.

'Are you sure, Gyles?' I asked.

'Absolutely Michael, Christine and Neil will love it.'

So I told them that Kenny More, star of such landmark films as *A Night to Remember*, *Genevieve* and *Reach for the Sky*, had always envied actors like Laurence Olivier, Rex Harrison and Stewart Granger. Kenny was the most unassuming actor; charming, modest and certainly not someone who would take his character home with him at night, as some actors do today. When he was filming the scene in *Reach for the Sky* where Douglas Bader looks under the sheets of his hospital bed and realises that both his legs have been amputated, I asked him what his motivation was during this harrowing sequence.

'To be honest, darling, we rehearsed it just before a tea break and my main concern was whether there would be any sandwiches left on the catering trolley by the time I'd finished.'

'So Kenny told me, "Actors can be split into two types – the shits and the c**ts",' I told the party. '"I wanted so much to be a shit like all those pushy, ambitious actors who made it to Hollywood. Larry was a bit of a shit, and so was Rex, and as for Jimmy Granger, well he invented the word, but I always ended up with the c**ts, propping up the bar at Pinewood Studios, doing British films for no money."'

Gyles laughed, Michèle laughed, Hilary laughed, Neil laughed. Christine did not laugh.

'I will not have that word used in my company. How dare you?' she bristled.

'I'm sorry, Christine, but I wasn't using it as a swear word,' I replied.

'I don't mind what you were using it for . . . you didn't need to use it at all.'

'Well, I did actually, Christine. It doesn't really work as a story if you don't.'

'So don't tell the story then. I think it's disgusting.'

'I thought it was quite amusing,' said Neil.

'Well I didn't,' said Christine, 'so let's leave it at that.' She returned to her fish pie.

A very divisive word, c**t. In England it can silence a room, in the USA it can clear a room and in Scotland it has a whole life of its own, where it is constantly used, not only as a noun but as a verb and an adjective. Best kept in asterisks though.

Molly had an early encounter with the 'c' bomb when she was six. She had been driven home by a parent friend, with whom Hilary shared a school run.

'Trisha used the "c" word in the car on our way home today,' Molly announced over family tea.

'The "c" word?' Hilary said.

'Yes, the "c" word Mummy.'

Hilary and I looked at each other in horror.

'I can't believe that,' I said. 'Mrs Pearlman is a bit offbeat but I can't believe she would have said that in a car full of children.'

'Well she did,' said Molly firmly.

Barney tucked into his beans on toast.

'Moll, would you spell out to me the word she used? I don't want Barney to hear it,' said Hilary.

'Sure,' replied Molly. 'C . . . R . . . A . . . P.'

Relief from her parents.

'I didn't believe she would have dropped the "c" bomb,' I said.

There was a pause. Barney looked up from his beans.

'Mummy?' he asked.

'Yes darling?' said Hilary.

'What's KEEP?'

Although he lived for a large part of his life in California, ending up in Rancho Mirage in Palm Springs with his third wife (the exotically named Baba Majos de Nagyzsenye), Patrick Macnee was a very regular correspondent. Had I been his agent during the days of the email, he would probably have been in touch with me on a daily basis.

Our first meeting in the early 1970s was not auspicious. He was appearing in a play called *Softly Goldfish Mating*, a light comedy, with the accent on the word 'light'. He had been a client of Laurie Evans, though Laurie was bored with him and had passed him on to me. I went to see the play in Wimbledon at the beginning of a pre-West End tour, but all was clearly not well. Pat was certainly not on top of his lines and was physically far from light in a role that called for a svelte leading man, lounging around in a fitted silk dressing gown, surrounded by a bevy of young beauties.

When I walked into his dressing room, Pat was

sweating heavily and in a very bad mood. Before he had a chance to tell me what a joy it was to finally meet and how nice to see me in Wimbledon, not to mention how grateful he was for my visit, he said, 'This play is a fuck-ing disaster', delivered in what I thought was quite an accusatory way. He was still in costume and I detected a paunch protruding from his snugly fitting dressing gown, which I hadn't noticed from the stalls seat he had arranged for me. What I had noticed, however, was that he was very breathless.

'I know I'm carrying a few extra pounds,' he said.

Had he read my mind?

'But I am finding the whole thing very exhausting. I hope to God we're not coming into the West End with it.'

I wanted to assure him that, having seen it, I could put his mind at rest on that score, but given that we had only just met, I thought that might sound a bit negative. The play didn't come into the West End and Pat returned to California. And a few weeks later, a note arrived from him.

'Just to let you know that I'm losing weight fast so that I can wear fitted dressing gowns on stage again,' together with a selection of photos of himself in underpants taken by him in front of a full-length mirror.

He didn't look to be much lighter than when we had met in his dressing room in Wimbledon, but at least he was trying. These updates continued to arrive on a monthly basis and he was clearly making good progress in shifting the pounds. And then one day, as I was leaving my office for lunch at The Garrick Club, a letter arrived from California. I put it in my pocket and opened it when I got to the club. There was no letter from Pat, just half a dozen photographs, again taken in front of a full-length mirror, but this time he was in the nude.

'Interesting photos,' said my guest, who had appeared behind me and was looking over my shoulder. 'Isn't that John Steed?'

I explained the background to the nude shots as I shoved the photos and envelope inside my newspaper. Then, having enjoyed several pre-lunch vodkas, some red wine and a couple of Kümmels on the rocks (this was the 1970s, remember), I completely forgot to pick up the newspaper from my dining-room chair after lunch.

A letter from the club secretary arrived a couple of days later.

Dear Mr Whitehall,

I believe the enclosed photographs, which were found in the Club yesterday, belong to you, and we thought that you would want them back.

Many years later, I came across a fan website for Pat, which said that 'in later life, he became an enthusiastic nudist', which naturally came as no great surprise to me. Mr Macnee was a great character and I suspect he carried off being a naturist with all the charm and grace that he displayed when fully dressed.

5

Pont Street Dutch

When Jack and Nora bought a pretty cottage on the Thames in Sonning (thinking that life in the country might be preferable to life in the suburbs), now famous for its celebrity residents including Theresa May and George and Amal Clooney, the house was called 'Rose Cottage', but Nora thought that was rather a common name and so changed it to 'Pilgrims', which she thought had more of an *à la carte* feel to it.

In spite of the name change, Nora never really settled in Sonning. When we moved in, the first thing she did was swathe the whole house in net. In front of the cottage there was a wide road, and all the houses on the opposite side nestled behind sizeable front gardens, so there was little chance of being overlooked. To the rear of the cottage, there was a long garden with tall trees at the end, so again nothing to see or be seen by, other than an inquisitive squirrel or blackbird. The main problem with having heavy net curtains in the cottage was that, with relatively small windows and plenty of lead and glass roundels, there was not a lot of light. So the whole place was usually in almost pitch darkness.

The back garden was attractive but overlooked on either side by our neighbours' gardens. We had a very distant relationship with both sets. Nora deemed the Horsleys to our left to be 'jumped up' and the Stourton-Smythes to our right 'too grand'. She was a difficult woman to please when it came to neighbours, although Jack did at least dissuade her from increasing the heights of our boundary fences from six to ten feet.

Village life didn't really suit Nora either, and Jack found the driving up and down to London every day exhausting. The lady who ran the village shop was sweet and helpful, but she and Nora had an early spat. After Nora questioned the provenance of some local gooseberries and then found a weevil in a bag of rice, which wrecked her plans for a rice pudding, she ended her patronage of the village shop. She was not a woman who refrained from bearing grudges.

My grandfather, Richard Ernest Baxter Whitehall, known as REB, who had made a lot of money in retail, was also no stranger to a spot of umbrage. He had never forgiven Nora for insisting that we were sent – at (his) great expense – to Ampleforth for a 'proper Catholic education'.

'What's wrong with the Whitgift?' he said.

'The Whitgift School is not Catholic and is in Croydon,' Nora replied.

'What's wrong with Croydon?' asked REB.

'I don't want the boys going to school in Croydon and that's the end of the matter.' Nora was always quite firm with REB despite the fact that he was coughing up all the money.

As REB had often decreed that Jack was no good with money, this was reflected in his last will and testament. Still smarting from having to pay our school fees, when he died he left his children – Cyril, Alice and Jack – a third share each, but with the proviso that Jack was only to get the interest from his share, not the capital. This was very unfair, as Jack's siblings both had plenty of money already. Then, on Jack's death, his capital was to be divided equally between all six grandchildren, thereby diluting it further. Poor Jack. But although he didn't get his hands on as much money as he thought he might, the extra bit of income meant that my parents could leave Sonning and move back to London. Although this time they would go somewhere considerably more *à la carte* than Beckenham.

Pont Street Dutch was a term coined by Osbert Lancaster to describe an architectural style typified by the large, redbrick, gabled houses built in the 1880s on Pont Street, just off Knightsbridge. Our new home, 44 Pont Street, ticked all the right boxes for Nora: a classy address in the royal borough; a large, second-floor flat in a tall elegant house; and within easy reach of Harrods, which in the early 1960s was a very different kettle of fish to the souk it is today. Nora loved Harrods, although she very seldom bought anything there. The house also had a lift, which Nora only used when it was not occupied. She managed to get through her entire stay at No. 44 without ever speaking to the neighbours, just giving them a shy smile from time to time.

While Jack was off flogging ladies' coats, suits and furs to various buyers at London department stores, Nora caught up with one of her old teachers from the Bromley School of Art, which she attended when we lived in Beckenham. Nora had always been a talented artist. When she left school she studied art at the Glasgow School of Art and, after graduating, got a job as a commercial artist with a Glasgow fashion house, sketching and painting the collections to send out to potential customers. She was clearly very skilled at painting figures and used this gift to develop a more personal interest in painting nudes. They were certainly very lifelike, but presented her with a problem as Barry and I grew up. She thought it inappropriate to have us in close proximity to pictures of naked men and, even worse, naked women, her Catholic sensibilities coming to the fore. So, before we came home for our school holidays, there would be a mad rush to – what Jack used to call

– 'dressing Mummy's nudes'. The problem with Nora's dressed nudes was that their outfits covered almost the entire painting. Nora chose to 'dress' them, usually in black, in very unflattering costumes. She always applied two coats of paint over sensitive areas to prevent Barry getting a flutter of excitement at the vestiges of a redacted nipple, or worse. No inadequate wisps across the lady's private parts for Nora: at least two coats of good Winsor and Newton oil were required in case my brother and I caught a glimpse of what was underneath.

Leonard Appelbee had been her teacher at Bromley. A relatively successful professional artist, he had studied at the Royal College of Art in the 1930s and Nora had clearly taken a shine to him. He even gave her the occasional lift home. And now, years later, Nora discovered that he lived just round the corner from our new flat, in Walton Street. She quickly made contact, very rare for her, and they picked up where they'd left off. Nora had regular weekly sessions when she would go to his studio to paint; although now she was more into landscapes and watercolours, which were much less trouble with regard to us. Leonard was something of a mystery figure; we were never to meet him, and Barry often wondered if perhaps there might have been more to these lengthy afternoon art sessions than just painting. It wasn't just the canvasses that she returned home with; there seemed always to be a spring in her step and a slight flush to her cheek – but this was probably just the overactive imagination of two teenage boys. In any case, after many productive months, Nora announced over breakfast that Leonard had left and gone to live and work in the West Country. She looked very sad; there could almost have been a tear in her eye. Jack was unconcerned. 'Best place for him,' he said. I always felt that she never had quite the same passion for her art after that, which was a shame, as I know it had given her so much pleasure. I suspect that she was like many women of her generation who, once they got married and had children, had to give up on all their hopes and aspirations. Their paths were laid out and there was little chance of deviating from them without dire consequences and social shame; something that I know she could not have contemplated. Looking back now, from my adult stand point and seeing how life is so different for my daughter Molly, I can quite understand why occasionally she had to let off steam.

One weekend there was a ring at the front door. Two young men wanted a word with Nora. American, with hats and raincoats, they were both suspicious-looking and very oleaginous. They told her they were Evangelist pastors and wanted to talk to us as a family. Barry went to his bedroom and locked the door; Jack went into the kitchen; and I didn't move quickly enough so was trapped in the sitting room with Nora and the oily Americans. Nora told Avery and Todd that we were Catholic, but that seemed to make them even keener to tell us more about their brand of faith, which seemed to involve being 'born again' and spreading the Christian message, repenting and turning away from sin. None of this remotely appealed to me, although Nora suddenly got very enthusiastic about the whole thing and called Jack in from the kitchen. She then made tea for us all.

When they'd left, Jack, Barry and I told Nora that we had all found them very creepy and that if they called again, we shouldn't let them in.

'Once you let those sorts of people into your home, you'll never get rid of them,' said Jack forcibly. (This came from the man who had hidden in the kitchen for most of their visit.)

When the creepy Evangelists returned a couple of days later, Nora ignored Jack's advice and invited them in and offered them a drink. When Jack returned from work, there was quite a party mood in the sitting room, no doubt aided by the large gin and tonics that Nora had dispensed. It was these that I was more interested in, rather than the early evening lecture on spreading the Christian message. Jack poured himself a triple measure, clearly cross that Nora had ignored his advice. Avery then suggested we kneel and say a prayer together.

Todd added, 'Why don't we all hold hands and close our eyes, so that we truly feel the presence of the Holy Spirit within us?' At this point the only spirit I was feeling within me were the two large Gordon's gin and tonics that I had consumed in quick succession, which had the effect of making me desperate for a wee.

'Dear God, please protect Mr and Mrs Whitehall and Michael from sin, and grant them salvation and faith in Jesus Christ,' intoned Avery as he swayed from side to side.

'And may we all meet, Jack, Nora, Michael, Avery and Todd as one family, in unison with God's holy will.'

This flicked a switch in Jack's head.

'What *family*?' He leapt to his feet and told them both to leave. I don't know if it was the drink that triggered this, or the fact that he was never a particularly religious man.

'Please Jack, we were hoping that you would say a prayer for us all,' replied Todd. 'Just in your own words.'

'That would be nice, Jack,' said Nora.

'The only words I shall be using are GET OUT OF MY HOUSE ... NOW!' he shouted as he pushed them towards the front door. This was a surprise to me as he was not a man who resorted to physical force very often, if indeed ever.

'But we were having such a wonderfully warm and happy time with you all,' said Avery.

The grandparents at Jack and Nora's wedding (Moneybags REB on the left). *(Author's collection)*

I wonder what all these dots and lines mean? *(Author's collection)*

Candy eyeing my parents and me up for lunch. *(Author's collection)*

Nora in artistic mode.
(Author's collection)

Nora and her brother Walter keeping their distance from Candy's gnashers. *(Author's collection)*

I was a shy and retiring boy. *(Author's collection)*

The Whitehalls at the Café de Paris hitting the champagne. *(Author's collection)*

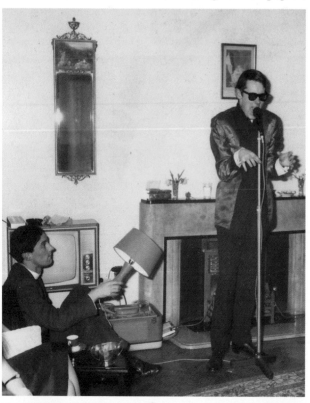

Barry helping me into the spotlight.
(Author's collection)

Slave labour. *(Author's collection)*

Charles Bonham
catching up
on the news.
(Author's collection)

All-purpose
Head of Games.
(Author's collection)

With a bevy of beauties. *(Author's collection)*

Keeping a firm hold on the current Mrs Whitehall. *(Author's collection)*

With Neil. Double denim: never a good look. *(Author's collection)*

Smoocher and fans. *(Author's collection)*

'Well, you're not any more. Get out and stay out,' he yelled, and slammed the door behind them.

Nora didn't speak to him for the rest of the evening.

'They were such sweet boys. What were you doing shouting like that?' she asked him afterwards. 'And it was very rude of you to shove them out so brusquely.'

I helped myself to a third gin and tonic, at which point Barry stuck his head round the door.

'Well done, Daddy,' he said. 'I thought they were total creeps.'

I often wondered if Jack had secretly wanted to shove Leonard Appelbee out of Nora's life like this, but had lacked the courage, so had taken it out on these two characters instead. Given that these sorts of topics were not up for discussion with Jack, who was not a man to share his feelings, I never got to find out.

6

A Man Among Boys,
a Boy Among Men

Balcombe Place was a modest boys' preparatory school in West Sussex, with much to be modest about. Geoffrey Teale had taken a lease on the house in 1954 and opened a school there, which he ran until 1969. It had previously been the headquarters of the Women's Land Army and later became a care home.

I arrived on the school's doorstep for the summer term of 1959, having been interviewed by Mr Teale at Gabbitas and Thring's offices in London a couple of weeks earlier. I was a late replacement for a geography teacher who had to leave for 'personal reasons', details of which Mr Teale hadn't disclosed to his educational agents in Sackville Street.

'A chap called Pratt. He came through us,' Mr Levy told me at the office before Mr Teale arrived for the meeting. 'Might have been for a bit of wandering hands,' he added. 'It's a Catholic prep school, as you know.'

Mr Teale was brusque as he showed me around the empty school a few weeks later, having offered me the job at seventy-five guineas a term. The boys were due to arrive the following day. He introduced me to Mrs Teale, a rather mousy, middle-aged woman with a very off-putting squint, one eye saying hello and the other, where are you?

'My wife is also the matron,' he said. 'She virtually runs the place, to be honest.'

When I had originally applied for this job, I was a little concerned about my lack of qualifications. I had A level English and history, but no degree and certainly no teaching qualifications.

'Teale is completely unqualified,' Mr Levy told me, 'so don't worry about that. You'll be in charge of geography, so you can be your own boss, which I doubt will be much of a challenge.'

There were only fifty-two boys in the school; I think there had been a few problems filling the beds. As it was the beginning of the summer term, Mr Teale asked me if I played cricket.

'I was 1st XI scorer for my old school, Ampleforth,' I told him. 'So I guess technically I scored more runs than anyone at the school.' Mr Teale shot me a disapproving look. He was clearly not a man with an ironic sense of humour, or indeed a sense of humour of any kind.

Later that day I met some other members of the common room, who, though not large in number, all seemed perfectly affable, if a little weird. Michael Keane, a geography and games master, was very charming, very tall, and wearing a very thick, faded tracksuit on a very warm early summer's day. The senior master Mr McShane – he never shared his Christian name with me or anyone else, but there was rumour that it was Claude – was senior in more ways than one and was in charge of classics. He'd recently retired from a minor public school, so had moved down a rung or two. He resembled an elderly mole and indeed had a large, hairy one on his cheek. I met the final member of staff in his bath; I wasn't actually in it with him, but we were sharing a two-bedroomed flat above the stables, with very modest bathroom and toilet facilities. When I first clapped eyes on him, he was lying in the bath, with the door wide open, his feet balancing on the taps, smoking a cigarette and reading a book of poetry.

'Do you like Ezra Pound?' he asked. I had no idea who Ezra Pound was. 'My favourite poet,' he continued, 'after T. S. Eliot.' I had no idea who T. S. Eliot was either. I would clearly need to find something else for us to have in common, I thought.

The character in the bath was Charles Bonham, head of English and recently graduated from Cambridge with a double first. He was yet to find his niche in life and was putting bread on the table by teaching. Pleasant looking, unruly hair and, as I discovered once he'd got out of the bath, by no means a snappy dresser, he had the look of an impoverished poet about him. (Perhaps he wanted to be the next Ezra Pound, whoever she was?) So no competition from him in the sartorial stakes, I thought, seeing as I had spent a considerable amount of time constructing the look of a schoolmaster for myself.

I had decided at nineteen that if I was going to be taken seriously as a teacher, and a head of department no less, I would have to abandon the look I had worked so hard to cultivate for myself in London, as a bit of a dandy: foulard silk scarves, drainpipe jeans, raffish suits, trendy ties and a jaunty Robin Hood felt hat with feather; all would have to be left at home with my parents. I had to strip away all style and think more geography teacher who was sleeping in his car as a result of going through a tricky divorce. So in came a crumpled Harris tweed sports jacket, one size too small, grey cords several inches too short, round spectacles broken on one side and repaired with sticking plaster, scuffed brown brogues in urgent need of a sole and heel, a stained woollen tie and a cheap pipe. This would be my new look, and I hoped would cover up my lack of qualifications.

Later that day the boys started to arrive. They were all dressed in grey Aertex shirts and grey shorts, topped by extremely camp grey sun hats. These sun hats were apparently Mrs Teale's idea, and, as so often with her ideas, not a good one. I was trying to discuss dormitories with the Teales, but I was having great difficulty keeping the St Bruno Flake alight in my pipe, which necessitated me continuously sucking and puffing on it. Unfortunately, all this achieved – beyond creating a thick cloud of smoke – was that I began to feel as sick as a dog, and light headed. I was forced to use Mrs Teale to steady myself a couple of times, which she was not pleased with at all, especially as she was also inhaling all the excess smoke caused by my efforts. I slipped a Geoff or two into the conversation, hoping we might get our relationship on to a slightly less formal footing, but this was met with frosty looks from them both. It was now clear that Mr Teale was not a Geoff or even a Geoffrey – well, certainly not to me he wasn't. I later discovered that Mrs Teale's Christian name was Brenda, though this was never used by any members of staff, apart from Mr McShane, after he'd got some Dutch courage aboard at the George and Dragon in Balcombe village.

I quickly realised that Mr McShane liked a drink, which usually led to several more. He also mixed his drinks, always a dangerous route to speedy intoxication. A couple of light ales to 'clear his palate' would be followed by sherry, before he settled into large gin and tonics. And then he would carry on after lunch in similar vein. As senior master he was in charge of the school rulebook, with which he seemed to be completely obsessed. And what rules they were.

Boys are not allowed to run up and down the drive from the playing fields to the main buildings.

Boys are forbidden to use the upstairs lavatories during the day.

Boys are not permitted to sing on the school premises, except in choir or chapel.

Boys are only allowed one biscuit each at teatime.

Boys are only permitted to write in blue ink. Fountain pens are to be used at all times. No ballpoint pens are allowed . . .

And on it went . . . on and on . . . and on. There were over fifty, and Mr McShane loved them all. I could see why, in the past, another word for schoolteacher was pedant. Pride of place in his study was the master copy of *The Balcombe Place Rule Book 1959*, and hanging on the back of his study door was a cane – one of those thin, whippy ones that make a swishing noise as they move through the air; although, to be fair, it seemed to be presented more as a threat, as I don't remember him actually ever using it.

I found my shared accommodation with Charles Bonham exhausting. Although a thoroughly charming and decent chap, he was a shambles. Full ashtrays, dirty socks and pants, wet towels, used teacups, empty beer bottles were littered everywhere. He seemed completely oblivious to his surroundings and his appearance, and was permanently covered in cigarette ash. And yet in spite of his academic prowess and love of American poetry, his other choice of reading was bizarre. He bought the *Sunday Pictorial* every week, reading it from cover to cover several times, and discarded copies of this lowbrow rag were littered around the floor of our 'set of rooms', as he rather grandly described our stable-yard accommodation. He was intellectually my superior and, unlike me, never needed to prepare his lessons or indeed give them a moment's thought. Charles's lessons were a flight of fantasy, packed with entertainment for the boys; he was one of those inspirational teachers who gave his pupils a lifelong love of literature. But in every other department he was a complete disaster. Indelibly etched in my memory is the sight of him lounging in our bath with a lit cigarette resting on the soap dish, a book propped up on the wire bath rack, eating cold baked beans out of a tin, off a very grubby comb.

One thing I took with me to Balcombe – which certainly enhanced my credibility with the boys – was my very chic, black, split-screen Morris Minor Convertible. The car had been bought for me by my loving parents, courtesy of REB, who thought that I needed to arrive at my new job in some decent transport and not in my beaten up Messerschmitt bubble car, which Barry had sold me at a knockdown price. The boys were offered trips around the village with the hood down in return for cleaning the 'Moggie' every weekend. Suddenly, this arrangement was stopped, much to the boys' dismay, when Mr McShane introduced a new rule to the 1959 rulebook, stating that: 'Boys are not allowed to accept lifts from members of staff in their cars, nor members of staff to offer them.'

'That's probably because Mr Pratt used to give us lifts in his car before he left,' a boy called Cockett told me later with a knowing look. Was that the scene of the crime, that had sent my predecessor packing?

On reflection, though, no bad thing, as what nobody knew was that I only had a provisional driving licence and should have technically had L-plates on the car. (Of course I wouldn't have dreamt of putting them on my beautiful Moggie, as they would have entirely ruined the *look*.) I did, however, take the assistant matron, Mary Wisbech, out a few times in it, and I think I might even have put my hand on her knee on one or two occasions, mistaking it for the gear stick. My mind drifted back again to Mr Levy's words about wandering hands. Thankfully she didn't seem to object but, being a good Catholic boy, I took it no further, and our friendship remained purely platonic. I was some years off discovering the joys of the opposite sex. Different times.

Boys can be cruel; teachers even worse. We used to sing this song to the tune of 'D'ye ken John Peel' on our way back from the village pub, when we knew Mr Teale wasn't around:

> Do you ken Geoff Teale in his white string vest,
> Ruining the school in the way he knows best,
> Do you ken Geoff Teale when he's far, far away,
> At the Oratory in the morning!

As the Oratory was the closest Catholic public school to Balcombe, Mr Teale tried, with varying degrees of success, to shoehorn as many boys into it as possible, working hard to maintain a close relationship with their headmaster. He wore a loose-fitting, cream string vest throughout the year and, as I had already established, he was definitely not a Geoff.

Towards the end of term, he hauled me into his study, and ranted at me for writing inadequate end-of-term reports. I had thought that, as long as I didn't use words that parents might think reflected on my teaching inadequacies, such as 'lazy' or 'stupid', I would be safe. I remember one school report I received at Ampleforth, which ended with: 'But all is spoilt by his blatant buffoonery.' My father unexpectedly told me not to worry and blamed the teacher for not keeping me under tighter control. So, when I started writing my own reports, I tended to be succinct but – in the main – complimentary. 'A good term's work', or 'A very good term's work', if I thought the boy had gone that extra mile, or 'Satisfactory' if I knew that he hadn't.

'This report is ridiculously short. The parents will expect considerably more than this, after the money they have spent on the fees,' said Mr Teale, as he handed me the report for a boy with the slightly unfortunate name of Badcock, in which I had written, 'A good term's work.' In another report for a boy called Organ, I wrote 'Organ is going to have to change his tune when it comes to getting on with his work.' Teale was furious and told me that writing reports was a serious business and I should refrain from making cheap jokes at the children's expense. I was just praying he didn't get to the one for Cockett!

'Far, far too short,' he blustered.

'How about, "Your son has worked very hard this term",' I suggested hopefully.

Mr Teale exploded.

I ended up writing a report that even Mr Teale thought was too long winded, and which opened with, 'Very few boys in my geography class have shown as much passion, unbridled enthusiasm, focus and fervour for oxbow lakes, which we have been studying this term, as your charming son has. I would say that he has an incisive and forensic mind when it comes to fine detail, and he is always first to put his hand up when there are house points to be earned. In fact, I would go further and say that Crutchley has the makings of a future geographer if he so chooses, and if he continues with this level of engagement, there is a whole raft of opportunities that could open up for him in the future, enhancing his career prospects no end . . .'

I think it was this report that made Mr Teale's mind up to dispense with my services the following term. Or perhaps he had got wind of the song we had written about him? Or perhaps it was because I called him 'Geoff'? Or maybe because he'd found out about the status of my driving licence? Whatever the reason, in 1969, Mr Teale retired and sold the school to a Mr Kevin Botting. (I wonder if he was a Kev?) It closed for good six years later.

Mr Bonham left teaching and became a poet.

7

'Matchmaker, Matchmaker'

After my father Jack died at the early age of fifty-nine (he had inhaled so much of Nora's cigarette smoke that emphysema sadly took him away well before his time), Nora rather withdrew into her shell. She was always very shy, but living alone without her beloved Jack forced her deeper and deeper into it. She lived in a flat in Mortlake, and I visited her at least once a week and took her out for lunch once a month.

She loved going to The Caprice. During one of these lunches, Princess Diana came into the restaurant and sat at the corner table favoured by celebrities and often referred to by regulars as the Harold Pinter table. Nora was deeply impressed, and on many of our subsequent visits she always kept a close eye on the table in the hope that Diana might make a return visit. Imagine her excitement when a few months later she did, although Nora was far too shy to look at her. She talked about Jack a lot and how she'd always disliked it when, working in ladies' fashions, he would park the van emblazoned with WESTCOAT & INTREX LADIES COATS AND SUITS outside our house in Beckenham – especially as she'd told one of our neighbours that he was a retired naval officer. She would always want to know how work was going, and whether I would ever settle down and get a proper job. 'Mucking around with actors,' as she referred to it, was certainly not what I should be doing with my life, nor what she had had in mind for me.

'Why don't you go back to the Bar?'

I explained that I had only done six months of articles as a bar student, so it wasn't just a case of 'going back' to it.

'But you'd make a lovely barrister, dear, and you'd be so handsome in a wig and gown. Or perhaps a doctor? You'd make a lovely doctor.'

Nora had a thing about doctors, having watched too many episodes of *Emergency Ward Ten* and *Doctor Finlay's Casebook*.

I told her that, now being in my late thirties, I was beginning to get a career going as an agent, and anyway I was far too squeamish to be a doctor. But she continued insisting, for many years, that I was far too good to be a theatrical agent. She even suggested on one occasion, that I'd make a lovely estate agent. God forbid.

That would then bring her on to her next favourite topic for discussion: to settle down with a nice Catholic girl and have children. This was many years before I married the current Mrs Whitehall, so I was a bit foot-loose. Nevertheless, Nora's stipulation that the young lady should be Catholic was bizarre. I was very seriously lapsed at the time and had been for years, especially since my divorce from my first wife Jane. As I had spent so much time at school attending religious services of one kind or another, Vespers, Matins, Benediction, Mass every day and twice on a Sunday, not to mention weekly confessions, I thought I'd banked up enough church-going credit for the afterlife. Consequently, I wasn't really running with a Catholic set, and certainly not meeting any Catholic girls. And children were very much only an aspiration at that point.

I'd been put off once by an old buffer lunching next to me on the members' table at The Garrick Club.

'Married?' he barked.

'Well, not actually at the moment, no,' I replied.

'Very wise, never took on a wife myself. Far too much trouble . . . could never see the point of it.'

'I'm about to get married though.'

He looked to me like a man who didn't know whether he was Arthur or Martha. A lot of neatly combed, dyed hair, and suspiciously tanned skin for February. I certainly didn't want him to think that I was in the Martha camp. I had once taken an American theatre director to dinner at The Garrick, and he had got terribly excited when he'd discovered that the club only had male members. He was crestfallen when he realised that this had nothing to do with their sexual orientation, which in his case was on the promiscuous end of gay.

'Trouble with wives is all they want to do is spend your money and breed,' said the buffer. 'Children cost a bloody fortune and it never stops. Wives are the same, and divorces. There's no end to it. Take my advice and keep clear of the whole fucking thing.'

This was very encouraging stuff for a would-be participant in a second trip up the aisle. I was now in my early forties, and Nora was forever reminding me, year after year, that I would make a wonderful father, but not if I left it too late.

'I know all those actors you do for, or whatever you call it (making me sound like a second-rate cleaner, rather than a leading show-business agent) are like your children. They certainly behave like children, and spoilt ones at that, but it isn't the same. You should think of yourself for once. I still don't understand why you muck about with them anyway; they're only interested in themselves. If only you could get yourself a proper job!'

I wasn't quite sure what I was doing having this conversation in my early forties with my eighty-year-old mother. I was beginning to feel like Anthony Perkins in *Psycho*, by coincidence a client at the time.

'Picasso fathered a child when he was eighty-two,' said Nora. 'So there's no reason why you shouldn't.'

Nora liked quoting Picasso endlessly, despite the fact that he was twice my age.

Nora's other obsession was that I saw more of my brother Barry. He was three years older than me, and had worked for the BBC since he left school in various administrative jobs; he had ended up as Controller of Resources. At one point he was running the BBC in the British Solomon Islands, which must have given him plenty of downtime. I was very fond of Barry, and he was my only sibling, but to describe us as close would be an exaggeration. He was always prepared to give me backroom support when I was showing off, but I don't think he ever really trusted me. When we were at boarding school together, he hardly ever spoke to me as I was his junior and consequently beyond the pale. He strongly disapproved of the fact that I regularly spent all my pocket money by the end of the first month of term and had to send SOS messages to Jack and Nora for replenishments (while he would return home with most of his money intact). Reliable, honest and dependable, Barry was perhaps a bit too much of a goody-two-shoes for me.

'I wish you boys got on better,' Nora would often say. 'He'd so like to be friends.'

Sadly we never really were – we were just so different.

(Fortunately this was never the case with my own children, due in very large measure to the fact that my two sons had a sister between them, and a sister who, like their mother, is a bit of a saint. She is the glue that binds them together.)

Nora never wanted to be any trouble, which often could be very annoying. I always wanted to send a taxi for her when we had our lunches together, but she insisted on coming by bus. And when I suggested that she came over for Sunday lunch, she'd always say that she didn't want to get in the way and was sure that I would much prefer to see one of my actor friends. A quiet Sunday with Stewart Granger (the only one of my clients that she ever got excited about) or Dorothy Lamour, perhaps? Poor Nora, she was never any trouble, apart from going on and on about being too much trouble.

Sadly, she had dementia in her late seventies and finally went into a home on Ham Common, where she received twenty-four-hour care. By then I was married (again) and baby Jack had arrived. He was born the year that she died, and I was so pleased that she got to cradle him in her arms, even if we did go round in circles conversation-wise.

Whenever the three of us arrived at the home, she would ask, 'Whose baby is this?'

'Mine, Mother.'

'Oh, you've had a baby at last, how exciting! What's her name?'

'It's a boy.'

'What a dear little chap. What have you called him?'

'Jack.'

'That's so lovely, to call him after your father. Dear Jack, he was a saint.'

Pause.

'So, why are you here?'

'We've brought Jack to see you.'

'Jack's here?' expecting Jack Senior to walk through the door in his wartime RAF uniform.

'No, baby Jack.'

'Baby?'

'Yes, I've had a baby.'

'You've had a baby? Oh, Jack would love to meet her. What have you called her?'

And on it would go. At least she had the repeated excitement of realising that I had finally had a baby. One of my great regrets was that she never got to meet Molly, who was born the following year. Nora had always wanted a daughter, and allegedly assuaged this disappointment by dressing me up in girls' clothes for the first few months of my life. (Fortunately without any lasting effects, though Jack Jr would dispute this.) She would have adored her.

And, although she wasn't a Catholic, she was thrilled that I had married Hilary.

*　　*　　*

The only skill I thought I might be capable of teaching my children was how to drive a car.

'Don't be ridiculous,' said Hilary, 'there is no way you could possibly teach anyone to drive, and certainly not any of our children. You lost your temper after five minutes trying to teach Jack to ride a bike, and if you remember you had Molly in floods of tears after her first lesson when you told her that bikes weren't really designed for girls to ride.'

'What I actually said was that girls weren't designed to ride bikes.'

'What, and that's a better way of phrasing it? You are unbelievable!' said Hilary. 'What century are you living in? It's 2006, for God's sake. Have you never heard of gender equality?'

'I don't know what you're talking about. But anyway, driving a car is a very different kind of skill,' I replied.

'Please don't let Daddy teach me to drive, Mummy,' said Molly. 'It would be all three-point turns and hand signals, and he wouldn't have a clue what any of the road signs meant.'

'Well, he had endless goes at trying to pass his driving test, so I certainly wouldn't recommend him as a teacher,' said Hilary.

It actually took me three attempts to pass the test. As I was approaching a zebra crossing in the Earl's Court Road, an elderly lady dragging a shopping trolley behind her took me by surprise, and I clipped the back edge of her trolley, dislodging a couple of items of shopping and causing her to momentarily lose her balance. When we got back to the test centre, the driving examiner told me that I had failed.

'Was that because of the incident on the zebra crossing?' I asked him.

'Yes, I'm afraid it was,' he said. 'If you hit a pedestrian on a zebra crossing, we have no alternative but to fail you.'

'But I didn't actually hit *her*,' I said. 'I only hit her shopping trolley.' The examiner clearly wasn't impressed with my explanation and he handed me the relevant document, confirming my failed test, which seemed to me to have been issued with rather more relish than was appropriate.

Six weeks later I had another go. As I got behind the wheel of the British School of Motoring Ford Anglia, I was relieved to discover that my examiner was considerably younger and less scary than my previous one, but worried that there was someone sitting in the back of the car.

'I hope you don't have any objections,' said the rather ominous man in the back, holding a large black clipboard, 'but I am assessing your examiner today.' So he was assessing my examiner, while the examiner was assessing me. My young examiner's mood changed abruptly as we drove off, and he became far less amiable. At the end of the test, it was obvious I was going to fail again. And just because I jumped a red light when I put my foot on to the accelerator mistaking it for the brake. A simple mistake, I thought, which I'm sure the examiner would have overlooked had he not had the sinister presence of the assessor in the back of the car.

Three months later I passed.

Tim, an actor client of mine and a good friend, had just split up from his long-standing girlfriend. Nobody could understand why. They were more married than most marrieds; maybe that was the problem, but it really didn't make any sense.

Janie was beautiful, charming, good fun and extremely bright. She was an editor at a publishing house, had extremely rich and attractive parents and lived in a very swish flat on top of their very swish house in Chelsea. Why didn't I ever meet anyone like that? With me, the girls I met who were beautiful were usually pretty charmless; the intelligent ones were plain and spotty, and the fun ones cost a fortune. And none of them had any money.

A few months after Tim and Janie split up, Tim started going out with Fiona. Fiona was a real Fiona: tall, toothy and far too talkative, but Tim was clearly smitten.

'Isn't she great?' he asked, not really looking for a response, when she left the table during lunch at Sheekey's.

'The bedroom department's incredible,' he continued. 'I've never had such amazing sex before.'

That was good to know, as I tucked into a main course of grilled langoustine.

Fiona certainly looked like a girl who would be very at home in Tim's bedroom; probably less so in the library and certainly not at all in the kitchen.

A couple of weeks later, Tim called me at my office and invited me to have lunch with him again. As he was one of a very small and extremely select group of clients who ever picked up a bill, I accepted immediately, despite being told that Fiona would be joining us. (The clients who invited me to lunch and then left me to pay were the most annoying; that well known fundraiser Bob Geldof was a past master at that particular ruse, as was Leslie Phillips, who would leave a bill on the table until it started to show early signs of foxing.)

'Fiona can't make it,' said Tim, 'she's having her hair done.'

Very Fiona, I thought.

As soon as we had ordered, we were talking about her again.

'What do you think of her, Michael?' he asked, this time sounding as though he *was* looking for a response, and a positive one at that.

'Well, to be honest Tim, I don't really know her. If you think about it, we've hardly seen each other socially since you started going out with her.'

'Hi, Michael!' said a voice behind me.

It was Lynne, an actress I used to represent. I introduced her to Tim, and we chatted. What a nice girl Lynne was, I thought. She'd be absolutely perfect for Tim.

'Let's meet up sometime,' she said as she went off to her table.

A few days later I called Tim.

'As you know, I'm not in the girlfriend market these days,' I said, 'but why don't you join Lynne and me for lunch?'

The Caprice was heaving, but we got the Harold Pinter table. Lynne was on sparkling form and looked ravishing. I engineered a phone call so that I could leave them together and even paid the bill.

I called Tim that evening.

'How did it go?' I asked.

'How did *what* go?' he replied edgily.

'Well, you and Lynne.'

'There isn't any me and Lynne, Michael. She's a typical actress, talked about herself all the time and thick as pig shit.'

That was rich coming from him. It sounded exactly like Fiona.

'Do you have a problem with me and Fiona?'

'A problem? What do you mean?'

'You don't really like her, do you?'

'Yes I do, I think she's great.'

'You preferred Janie, didn't you?'

'Janie was very different.'

'So you did prefer her.'

'Not particularly.'

'Look, Michael, be honest and tell me what you really think of Fiona. I'd value your opinion and I know you'd tell me the truth.'

'I've told you, Tim, I think she's great.'

'Please don't keep saying the same thing. Just tell me what you really think.'

I paused for breath. Well, why not? I didn't want Tim to think that I was incapable of having an opinion, although I did remember what had happened to poor Mary Evans when she'd offered Rex Harrison her candid opinion. But Tim wasn't Rex.

'Well, to be honest, Tim, I don't really think she's good enough for you.'

'What do you mean "good enough"?'

'Well, I guess I just think you could do better.'

'What, you mean Lynne is *better*?'

'Well, yes, I suppose I do.'

'Michael,' he replied. 'Why don't you ... why don't you ... mind your own fucking business!'

'Oh charming. You ask for my opinion, and when I give it to you, you start swearing at me.'

'So why do you think Fiona's not good enough for me? Some people probably think Hilary's not good enough for you.'

(Hilary seemed to be entirely irrelevant to this conversation.)

'Let's leave this, Tim, shall we? Hilary and I are going out to dinner. I'll call you in the morning.'

'No, don't run away, tell me why you don't like her.'

'I've never said I didn't like her.'

'Yes you have!' he shouted.

'Calm down, Tim! All I'm saying is I just wonder whether . . .'

'What?'

'Nothing.'

'What? Please Michael!'

'Well, I just wonder whether she's a bit . . . well . . . tarty.'

'Tarty!' he shrieked. 'Fiona tarty! She's the most *un*tarty person I've ever met.'

'Well I . . .' I sensed this wasn't going at all well; indeed Rex would probably have shown less aggression.

'And coming from you of all people . . . *tarty*.'

'Well, you did say . . .'

'Why don't you just go and fuck yourself,' he said, slamming down the phone.

I never saw Tim again, apart from very occasionally on television (he was not an easy sell). He and Fiona got married six months later, have three children and apparently, without my help, have lived happily ever after.

Oh, and they're not called Tim and Fiona.

I got involved in some more matchmaking, with similarly disastrous results, a year or so later.

Hilary's friend Louise was not enjoying life as a single mother. Her dentist husband had left her with a twelve-year-old son and gone off with his dental nurse, and Louise was feeling lonely and unloved. She had read in the paper that Ian Ogilvy had recently split up with his wife. Knowing that I was his agent, Louise asked if I could engineer dinner with him one evening.

'Ian is so attractive,' she said, 'and very much my kind of man.'

I also knew that Louise wasn't going to be Ian's kind of woman, so I tried to steer her off Ian and on to another recently divorced client of mine, Nigel Davenport.

'Ian's a bit of a "love 'em and leave 'em" type,' I lied. 'You've just divorced one of those. Nigel's more of a family man but still very attractive.'

I said 'still', because Nigel was ten or fifteen years older than Louise and, judging by some of his more recent relationships, had more modest aspirations than Ian.

I called Nigel.

'Hilary has a great friend called Louise, who is a fan of yours and would love to meet you,' I said. 'Very attractive and recently divorced. How about making up a foursome for dinner one evening?'

Nigel couldn't wait.

He had recently made a mess of an interview I had got him with an American film director and was now down in the dumps. The casting director had suggested Nigel to him for a supporting part in a Harrison Ford picture shooting in Europe. Nigel was a bit miffed that the producers had only sent him the pages in which he appeared, rather than the whole script.

'I need to get the feel of the whole film, not just my part,' said Nigel, overlooking the fact that his part was contained within six pages and had nothing whatsoever to do with the rest of the movie. In fact, it didn't really need to be there at all.

'So tell me about yourself?' asked the director.

'What do you want to know?' said Nigel tetchily. He had been waiting for over an hour in a very crowded office reception area off Lower Regent Street. There seemed to be a lot of people up for this part and Nigel wasn't accustomed to being interviewed for jobs; they were usually offered to him over the phone.

'Well, let's start with your name,' said the director.

'What . . . you don't even know my name?' said Nigel. 'Didn't my agent send you a CV?'

'Yeah, he probably did, but I've only just flown in from LA and I haven't had a chance to look at any CVs yet. Anyway, just tell me about yourself, what have you been up to?'

'What, you mean this morning?' He was getting annoyed.

The director kept going.

'Any recent movies?'

'I took my agent and his wife to see *Prospero's Books* last night. They didn't understand a word of it.'

'What's your name again?'

Nigel stood up, walked around the table and eyeballed the director.

'How dare you ask me to come to an interview, not bother to read my CV and not even know my name? Who the fuck do you think you are, you patronising American prick?'

Nigel then grabbed the lapels of the director's jacket and shook them.

At this point, the casting director appeared.

'I'm sorry I'm late, terrible traffic. So, you and Nigel have met?'

'I now know he's called Nigel,' said the director, having been lifted to his feet. 'Nigel, would you be kind enough to get your hands off me.'

The casting director realised the meeting wasn't going well.

The director shoved Nigel out of his way, which Nigel didn't appreciate, and he grabbed the director's lapels again. Nigel then took a swing at him, missed and fell back across the table.

'Get this clown out of here,' the American said to the casting director and stormed out of the room.

Later that afternoon, I called the casting director.

'How did Nigel's meeting go?' I asked.

'Not well,' she said.

'They didn't like him?' I asked innocently.

'No, unfortunately not. In fact Nigel tried to punch the director.'

Unlike him to have missed, I thought.

A couple of days later, Mrs Whitehall, Louise and I met Nigel at La Poule au Pot in Ebury Street – a perfect, romantic location with plenty of warm candlelight and cosy velvet banquettes – at eight o'clock. By eight thirty Nigel hadn't arrived and Louise was getting twitchy. Was Nigel going to stand her up? Was Nigel going to stand us all up?

And then the glass double doors flew open and in burst an unsteady and dishevelled-looking Nigel. The waiter led him over to our table.

'Sorry I'm late!' he shouted. 'Bloody cab driver took me to some Indian restaurant in Olympia. I could do with a drink.'

A drink looked like the last thing Nigel could do with.

'This is Louise,' said Hilary, as Nigel gave her a watery kiss and slumped down on to the banquette next to her.

I poured some wine into Nigel's glass. He looked more than a little below par: tie a bit wonky, hair a bit sticky-uppy, unshaven and generally nothing like the dashing Duke of Norfolk in *A Man for All Seasons*, which Louise had watched the previous evening in an attempt to bone up on his film career.

Nigel swilled down a couple more glasses of the Mâcon-Lugny and then we ordered. The three of us had steaks and Nigel had the duck *à l'orange*.

'Are you working at the moment?' said Louise, wisely thinking that the best topic of conversation for Nigel, while awaiting his duck, would be Nigel.

'No, it's all as dead as a doornail, isn't it Michael?' he replied, throwing me an accusatory glance.

'I couldn't even get a bit part in a Harrison Ford film. God protect me from over-sensitive American directors.'

By the time the food arrived, the conversation was grinding to a halt. Nigel attacked his duck *à l'orange* with passion, helped on by a few more glasses of wine, but hit an unexpected lump of bone, causing shards of orange-covered duck to shoot off his plate and on to the white tablecloth. At the same time, some of the sauce started to slither out of the corner of his mouth and down on to his shirt collar.

Louise handed him her napkin. 'I think you need a wipe down,' she said.

At this point, Nigel had a violent sneezing attack and more orange sauce shot out of his nose and across the table, a fair amount of it landing on the front of Louise's silk blouse.

Nigel apologised profusely and started to wipe the front of her blouse with his sodden napkin, making things even worse.

Louise leapt up from the banquette, excused herself and headed for the loo.

'Would you like water?' the waiter asked Nigel, having surveyed the carnage.

'No thank you, water is for washing, but another bottle of that Mâcon-Lugny would be very welcome.'

On her return, Nigel apologised to Louise again and she gave him a charming smile. Taking this as a long-awaited signal for a little intimacy, he slipped his hand on to her knee. As his hand was still covered in moist duck and sticky orange sauce, this caused Louise to leap up again and tell Nigel to keep his hands to himself. Our matchmaking dinner was going from bad to worse.

Louise decided it was time for her to head home. I offered to get her a cab.

'I'll give you a lift home,' said Nigel, clearly forgetting that he had not only drunk several bottles of white burgundy, but also didn't have a car.

'No, I wouldn't hear of it Nigel,' said Louise, 'I live miles away.'

'Where?' he asked.

'Wimbledon.'

'Wimbledon's on my way home.'

Nigel lived in Knightsbridge, and certainly nowhere near Wimbledon.

'No really, Nigel, I'll be fine.'

At which point Nigel went into aggressive mode. He blew his nose, straightened his tie and in a very loud voice said: 'In which case, I'll fuck off, which is clearly what you all want me to do . . .' He weaved out of La Poule au Pot, followed by several pairs of incredulous eyes.

As Hilary and I put Louise into a taxi, we apologised for the whole disastrous evening.

'No, it was great fun,' said Louise. 'I've never met a famous actor before.'

8

Saint Hilary

'It's not easy living with a saint' is a much-used phrase in the Whitehall home. It is usually delivered in the heat of the moment, mid-rant, when Hilary has behaved in her predictably perfect, saint-like and extremely aggravating manner. Living up to her standards of always doing and saying the right thing at the right time can be exhausting; it is a battle I gave up on long ago, as I was never going to achieve the Olympian standards that she expected of me. In this department we are so mismatched, it's a miracle that we have survived over thirty years of marriage. It wasn't the first time that I have found myself living with a saint, as my father Jack was definitely cut from the same cloth as Hilary when it came to saintly demeanours.

Of course, I know she is right, but some elements of her saintly behaviour are not easy to live with. If she can shoehorn a charitable element into anything, she will. No street beggar is ever passed without coins being tossed into his hat, and if a dog is in the vicinity of the hat, there will be a doubling up of the donation. While all this general goodwill-to-all-men is taking place, I am invariably waiting at the open door of a black cab with the meter running. We have diametrically opposed views when it comes to taking in deliveries for the neighbours. When I answer the door to a courier asking if I will accept a parcel for the neighbours, they are invariably met with a curt, 'No, sorry, I don't want to be tripping over their stuff for days, thank you very much.' Whereas Hilary is more than happy to let the neighbours use her as an unpaid concierge service, filling out their delivery details with our address and certainly never asking for her prior agreement to these arrangements.

'It says delivery at number six here on this parcel,' announces the charmless man from Parcelforce, who has had to ring our doorbell twice.

'Nice if number seven had asked us first. We'd have made sure we were waiting for you at the door,' I reply

Regarding tradesmen, Hilary will know not just their names, but also the names of their wives, children, dogs and probably in-laws; they will invariably be offered tea and biscuits before their tool bags have even hit the floor. The other day she asked the man servicing the boiler, who wanted a glass of water, whether he would like 'still or sparkling', and to the answer 'sparklin', please' added, 'with ice?' They are frequently given marriage guidance or childcare advice as they work, and it's a given that she will have their entire life story by the end of the job. I, on the other hand, won't even know what trade they practise or what they are doing in the house, let alone their names.

And don't get me started on Christmas and – more specifically – cards. Hilary's Christmas-card list is beyond parody and includes random characters going back to people we met on our honeymoon in 1987. A lorry driver and his wife from Wisbech have been particularly avid correspondents over the years, not to mention neighbours from the various houses we have lived in, teachers and parents from every school attended by our children, at vast expense, and even an American couple, the Lindens, who we met at our antenatal classes and whom we have never seen since. This might well explain why Hilary has nine godchildren and I have none.

To this day, the Lindens' annual Christmas card is always the first to appear, together with a photographically enhanced round robin; all those gurning faces and plain attendant children – why is it that unattractive people always overbreed? Hilary is, not surprisingly, a fan of the Christmas round robin. Equally unsurprisingly, I am not. If I can get to the post first, the letter element will never see the light of day. If only I could somehow fit a shredder to the letterbox during the season of goodwill. Hilary, however, persists in sending them out, but at least she never bragged about our children's A level results and university degrees – apart from our daughter Molly's, of course.

And then she is always willing to extend a helping hand to anyone trying to get into the entertainment industry, regardless of any talent. On many an evening she can be found in a thirty-seater fringe theatre above a pub, watching an unintelligible play written by a friend's child. Endless no-hopers have been introduced to agents and voice coaches. She has helped with speech choices for drama school auditions, given endless advice on who to write to and has read countless unsolicited scripts, about which she will always try to find something positive to say. Many a duff script, sent with a handwritten note to Eric Fellner and Tim Bevan, producers of *Four Weddings and a Funeral* and *Notting Hill*, whom Hilary has never met or spoken to in her life, has been diverted by me into the office shredder. If only she had wanted to be an agent, she could have earned 10–15 per cent out of all of these good deeds, but sadly saints don't earn commission. On the other hand, my advice to anyone wanting to be an actor or actress is always the same – don't.

Another aspect of Hilary's kindness has blossomed with Jack's success. When he is on tour, tickets are distributed like confetti, and his 'meet and greets' around the country are populated with what he and I call *Friends of Mummy's*, some more bizarre than others. Jack ran out of post-show conversation at the O2 very early on with the man he described as 'having had a camera up my father's arse.' I don't remember at what point during my colonoscopy appointment Hilary managed to discuss my gastroenterologist's ticketing requirements for Jack's show, but she clearly did. Another odd one Jack encountered was a girl in Cardiff who, when asked by Jack what her connection to Hilary was, replied, 'I cut your uncle's hair.'

'But he lives in Oxford; that's quite a commute you've got there,' he said, as he wondered how this girl had ever got into his mother's orbit. Other invitees include the butcher (a particularly good friend of Hilary's, although inclined to heckle at live shows), the coach driver who collects and delivers other people's children to rowing practice outside our house on Putney Embankment (but with whom we have no other connection of any kind) and an overzealous lady whom she met on a breast-feeding training course, invited by Hilary to a recording of *Live at the Apollo,* who droned on for hours to Michael McIntyre, having cornered him in the VIP bar afterwards, about how she 'could tell from his comedy that he was breast-fed.' Then there are the distant relatives, godchildren, unit drivers from past TV series, a very annoying man and his heavily pregnant girlfriend, who was the manager of the Big Yellow Storage where we had a unit briefly, and even the odd special-needs distant cousin, who is probably not a cousin at all.

Hilary has a saintly sidekick in her friend and Molly's godmother, Anne Mullins. They are co-conspirators in any charity fundraising operation. Long-term residents of Barnes and Putney have been known to dart down alleyways or hide inside the nearest shop when they see them both bearing down on them, waving flags and rattling tins. No local philanthropic venture would ever get off the ground without their wholehearted support. As fairy-godmother-in-chief, over the years, Anne has spared no expense on the presents she has lavished on her goddaughter. Sadly, these have usually been items on my personal hate list, such as high heels, hot pants, items made of Lycra, platform boots, boob tubes – (I believe this is how they are referred to, although Molly was not over-endowed in that department and they often ended up on eBay (a favourite method in the Whitehall family of moving on unwanted gifts) – and even, behind my back and unnoticed by me for several years, for her thirteenth birthday, pierced ears. Anne has a doctorate in philosophy and would conduct long-distance tutorials with Molly via Skype. So when she got her degree and it came time for her graduation ceremony, for which there were only two tickets available, I did the gentlemanly thing and stepped aside for Anne. By a strange coincidence, both Hilary and Anne wore bright orange to the ceremony, which caused the official photographer to ask Molly, as they reached the head of the queue, 'Would you like both your mothers in one photograph, or do you want separate pictures with each of them?'

'Catherine's husband has just lost his job again, and I said we would go round and cheer them both up.' Why would I want to go and 'cheer up' some loser husband friend of Hilary's, whose only connection to me is the fact that we have both chosen to live in the same London borough and our wives happen to walk their dogs together? Geoff was a crashing bore, and I wasn't at all surprised that he had lost his job. The greatest surprise was that he managed to get one in the first place.

Dog walking affords Hilary limitless opportunities to socialise with people who always appear to be lifelong friends of hers, whilst being total strangers to me. Who are these people? She knows their names, their dogs' names, their husband's names, their children's names and even which schools they go to. My sole contribution to these outings, if indeed I join her (it seems to me that one person is more than enough to walk a dog) is to ask her, 'Who the fuck was that?' as they walk off.

Humans are not the only ones who benefit from her care: animals also bask in her kindnesses. A plethora of pets have joined our family over the years, including dogs, who of course had to come from Battersea Dogs Home, and could only be addressed in a baby voice, not shouted at and certainly never smacked. And then there were elderly rabbits and guinea pigs rescued from various schools; a crested canary with a withered foot, which had difficulty staying on its perch and had languished in the local pet shop for months because nobody wanted it; love birds that were given to Molly by a boyfriend, in an ill-thought-out romantic gesture, which she palmed off on her mother when she and the boy split up and she didn't want to be reminded of the heartache. Unfortunately they became very aggressive towards one another and had to have a second rehoming by the local pet shop. Endless hamsters, most of whom escaped and ended up under the floorboards, where they died a slow death, leaving the most grisly smell. The hamster that lingers in the memory most is the one that had a hereditary malocclusion, which meant that her top teeth continued to grow and needed to be clipped periodically. After several expensive trips to the vet, Hilary asked him to show her how to do it herself. The sight of her wrestling with a wriggling hamster in one hand and a set of wire clippers in the other was not a pretty one.

On another occasion we were driving back from lunch in the country when we saw a dead cat in the middle of the road. As we passed, it moved its tail. Of course Hilary ordered me to pull over, so that she could investigate. I pointed out that there was nothing we could usefully do for a dead cat and that it was clearly a Lazarus reflex; but the look Hilary shot me made me realise that further resistance was futile.

'We have to do something,' she said.

'Reverse over it?' I suggested helpfully. She did not dignify this with a response and, instead, got out of the car. A few minutes later she returned carrying the 'dead' cat. Why couldn't she just have left it where it was?

'We have to find a local vet, so they can put it out of its misery,' she said.

'Oh, for God's sake, Hilary, just put it back. I am not having it messing up the car. I spent a fortune having it valeted yesterday.'

'Really, Michael, have some compassion! I'll have a look in the boot and see if there is anything I can put it in.' She rootled about for a minute and then got back into the passenger seat, carrying the cat in a carrier bag that she had found. I glanced at it as she placed it on her lap.

'Ironic that the only thing you could find to put a dead cat in was a Waitrose Bag for Life,' I said as I drove off.

'Not funny, Michael.'

On our way to the vet, the state of shock that the cat had clearly been in suddenly and unexpectedly wore off, and it sprang back to life, shredding the Bag for Life to pieces with its claws, and then jumped up on to the front dashboard, hissing and baring its teeth whilst continuing to slash with its claws. I stopped the car and both of us leapt out, slamming the doors.

'You'll have to go back in and turn the engine off,' said Hilary.

'No fucking way!' I replied. 'It was your stupid idea to stop and pick it up. If you'd let me reverse over it like I wanted to, it would have been well and truly out of its misery by now.' Another remark not well received.

'The phone's still in there. I need it to call the vet.'

'Good luck,' I said as she moved towards the door.

Unfortunately, the cat kept hurling itself at the window, spraying blood all over the inside of the car.

'I have to get that phone,' she said, 'otherwise we'll be here all weekend. You distract it and I'll go round the other side and see if I can snatch it out the other way.'

I did as instructed and, after three attempts, she managed to wrest the phone out of the car, even if she didn't manage to switch the engine off. I called the vet.

'You'd better make sure we don't get stuck with the bill for this bloody cat,' I muttered.

After a very long hour, during which the inside of my beautiful Mercedes was starting to look like the set of a

Quentin Tarantino movie, a young lady appeared. She didn't look old enough to be a vet, but what she lacked in age, she made up for in chutzpah. She manhandled the hysterical cat out of our car and into a cage. 'Don't worry, we'll make sure he gets the best possible care,' she said as she disappeared into her van.

'That's a weight off my mind,' I said.

Perhaps the most dramatic example of Hilary's saint-like behaviour came late one night when she was lying next to me during one of her insomniac moments. Suddenly we heard a piercing scream coming from the river.

She rushed to the open window and peered out of it.

'Help me, please! I'm in the water and I'm dying,' came a voice. Hilary turned to me.

'What should we do?'

'Shut the window?' I ventured. Advice that, needless to say, she ignored.

'Hold on, I'm coming,' Hilary shouted, as she put on a T-shirt.

I hadn't quite grasped what was going on.

'Phone the police, Michael, there's someone in the river,' she shouted as she ran down the stairs.

'Where is your wife now?' asked the policeman on the other end of the phone.

'I'm not sure, I think she's in the middle of the Thames trying to rescue some woman.'

'And where are you, sir?'

'I'm in my bedroom.'

'I see . . .'

'The point is, I can't swim so I wouldn't be much use down there, so I thought it would be best if I directed proceedings from up here.'

'Well, the patrol car is on its way. You stay put in case we need to call you back.' An instruction I reluctantly agreed to follow.

I shouted the news down to Hilary.

'Bring some towels, Michael,' came the reply.

Given the policeman had told me to stay put, I woke Molly, gave her some towels and told her to go and help her mother.

By now Hilary had got to the slipway.

'Do you need help?' she shouted at the woman flailing around in the river.

'Yes, I'm dying.'

She walked into the icy cold water. She later told me that, as she waded out, she was worried that the drowning woman might be luring her into some sort of trap and that they could both end up underwater, the vicious Thames current sweeping them away to their deaths. When she reached the woman, who fortunately, due to the tide being out, was just within her depth, she saw that she was floating on her back, fully dressed in a padded parka coat, jeans and UGG boots. As Hilary grabbed her, the woman looked her in the eye, repeated that she was dying and rolled on to her front, face down in the water. Hilary flipped her back over.

'Not on my watch you're not!' she barked, and dragged her slowly, face up, in the direction of the shore.

As they returned to the slipway, Molly appeared with the towels.

'Here are the towels from Daddy,' she said.

'Sorry, Molly, I know this is an emergency, but I am not ruining our best white Egyptian cotton bath towels. Go and get some others.'

'Yes, I thought they were an odd choice. Typical Daddy, not a clue!'

'And see if you can find the dog, she's run off.' Hilary multitasking as usual.

The police arrived minutes later and quickly discovered that the woman had mental health issues and had been sectioned. As I watched her from the window being driven away in the police van, I thought to myself that – even though it wasn't hugely dangerous – I admired my wife for her bravery. Always good in an emergency, Hilary.

We never did get our towels back, so just as well Molly had swapped them for Barney's rather garish football ones.

'I might try and find out where they've taken her, so that I can visit and make sure she is OK,' said Hilary, as she dried off after her river adventure.

'Well if you do, please don't put her on any guest lists

for Jack's future shows,' I said firmly. I know how my wife's mind works.

I had hoped that my children would be supportive of my attempts to rein in Hilary's excesses but, of course, it soon became clear that I was not going to get any help from that quarter, as they themselves squeeze every ounce of altruism out of her. But, without being overly uxorious, I'm extremely fortunate in having a saintly wife, considerably younger and fitter (in both senses of the word) than me and prepared to put up with me swearing at the television and banning her from watching programmes that are probably far more entertaining than *The Antiques Roadshow* and *Question Time*, but just not my kind of thing. Maybe I should be kinder to her and pretend I'm actually enjoying *One Born Every Minute* and *Paul O'Grady's For the Love of Dogs*.

9

'Making Plans for Nigel'

My second serious attempt at producing a TV drama series was in the early 90s. *The Good Guys* starring Nigel Havers and Keith Barron. LWT were looking for a new project with long-running potential for Nigel following his success in *The Charmer*. Lying in the bath one evening and wondering how I was going to pay the school fees, I came up with the idea of a show called *The Good Guys* featuring two accidental heroes who were both called 'Guy'. Unfortunately, at the time I pitched the project to Nick Elliott over the crispy duck and watercress salad at The Ivy, that's all I had.

I was very surprised when Nick came back to me the following day with an uncharacteristically encouraging response, and asked me to come over to his office. He'd spoken to Greg Dyke, then Controller of Programmes at LWT, who thought it was a great idea, was a big fan of Keith Barron and thought that he and Nigel would work really well together.

Nora with her freshly-minted grandson. *(Author's collection)*

Havers & Whitehall on the set of *The Good Guys*. *(Author's collection)*

Barney the bookworm. *(Author's collection)*

Hugh to Barney: 'The pork pie for tea is this big.' *(Author's collection)*

Hanging out with Neil in Perthshire.
(Author's collection)

Molly with her two mummies.
(Author's collection)

Bad hair day on *The Million Pound Drop*. *(Author's collection)*

The Whitehalls backstage after the Royal Variety Performance. *(Author's collection)*

Hogging the spotlight. *(Courtesy of Tiger Aspect/BBC)*

(above left) Nick Hewer auditioning for my part in *Backchat*.
(Author's collection)

(above right) From the cutting room floor.
(Author's collection)

(left) The St. Hilary Flood Rescue Service.
(Author's collection)

Carry on Cruising. *(Author's collection)*

Photobombed by Mr Seagal's manager. *(Author's collection)*

Mixing with the natives. *(Author's collection)*

Getting the lowdown on
Buddhism. *(Author's collection)*

Overdressed author by pool. *(Author's collection)*

'I'm still a bit light on detail,' said Nick.

'Well it's a comedy thriller really,' I replied. 'These two men, both called Guy, crash their cars into each other.'

'Nice,' said Nick. 'Then what?'

'Well the Havers Guy has a flat in Richmond and invites the Barron Guy to come and stay with him for the night.'

'They're not gay, are they?'

'No, no Nick, it's not the gay guys. Well, they could be if you wanted them to be?'

'No, I don't want a gay series, Michael.'

'OK, Keith's Guy lives up north and has just left his wife, and Nigel's Guy has just split up from his girl-friend, so they are a perfect fit.'

'And then what?'

'Well then . . .'

'What do they actually do?'

'Well, that's what the series is all about, Nick. They get involved in things.'

'Do you have a script?' Nick asked hopefully.

'Not at the moment.'

'Do you have a treatment?'

'Yes.'

'Who's written it?'

'Mmm . . . Jeremy Burnham?'

'Can I see it?'

'I . . . I don't have it with me.'

'OK, so send me a copy tomorrow and send one to Greg too. We have a network meeting next week, and if we're going to get this commissioned we need to move fast.'

'Fast is fine by me,' I replied confidently.

When I got back to my office, I tried to work out a plan of campaign. I hadn't really got much of a concept, I hadn't got a treatment, I hadn't got a script, and I certainly didn't have a writer. My friend Jeremy Burnham was just the first name that had come into my head, as I'd met him the previous week. I made the call.

'What are you doing at the moment?' I asked hopefully.

'I'm doing a script for the BBC and waiting to hear back from Granada about rewrites.'

'Well, you know that Nigel Havers, Keith Barron series idea I told you about . . .'

'Yes, *The Good Guys*, you said you'd got a writer set for it.'

'Yes . . . actually the writer who was going to do it has had a stroke and has had to pull out.'

'What, John Fortune's had a stroke?' asked Jeremy.

'Oh, did I mention John? No, he's in the middle of moving house and can't cope with any more pressure.'

'So who had the stroke?'

'Look, Jeremy, all I need at the moment are a couple of pages for Nick. You know what he's like.'

'I don't actually, because I don't think they like me at LWT. Well, Greg Dyke certainly doesn't.'

'I'm sure he does, Jeremy. Anyway, they were very positive about you doing it.'

'So when do they need it by? I'm pretty snarled up until Christmas.'

'Actually, I need it by tomorrow morning . . .'

'By tomorrow?'

'I think if I can get a strong selling document over to Nick by tomorrow lunchtime and Greg likes it, we could be in business.'

'Greg loved the treatment, and so did I,' said Nick on the phone a couple of days later. 'And you have definitely got Nigel and Keith attached, haven't you? Greg was very insistent on that.'

'Of course I've got Nigel and Keith, I'm their agent.' I made a mental note to self, 'Must tell Nigel and Keith about this.'

'There's only one small problem. Greg doesn't think Jeremy Burnham is the right writer for it. How committed are you to him?'

'Oh, not at all, Nick,' I said. 'He wrote that outline some time ago and I was probably going to bring in another writer anyway.'

The Good Guys was due to start filming the following spring with John Fortune, another client, as the lead writer. I rang John to see how the script was going for the opening episode.

'You find me at my desk,' he said confidently from his new house in Harlow, which he shared with his wife Deborah.

'How's the script going, John? You know we only have six weeks or so before pre-production.'

'I'm on page twenty-seven,' he replied.

The first draft script would probably be about sixty pages, so at least he was about a third of the way through.

'You'll definitely have it by the end of next week.'

I rang John a couple of weeks later.

'You find me at my desk.'

'How's it going, John? I was expecting something last week.'

'Yes, sorry about that, but Deborah is ill and I've been in and out of Harlow General all week. But I'm on page forty-five, so you'll definitely have it by the end of the week.'

I called him on the Friday.

'I'm on page fifty-three. Nearly there,' he said.

Half an hour later, the phone rang. It was Deborah.

'I'm so sorry to hear that you've been unwell,' I said.

'No, I'm fine. I just had a beastly cold for a couple of days. Look, I felt I ought to tell you something, Michael. It's about John's script . . .'

'Is John there?'

'No, he's gone to the pub, which is why I am phoning you now, but please don't tell him I have.'

'So what's happened?' I said.

'Well, it's more a case of what hasn't happened. I felt I ought to tell you . . . how can I put this . . . well . . . I'm afraid he hasn't . . . hasn't . . . written a line.'

John owned up the following day to Deborah's illness. It was all in his head, but he was finding it difficult to get it on to the page, and Deborah's cold wasn't helping the situation. I sensed another excuse building up. We decided to bring John up to Twickenham Studios under armed escort and lock him into a dark room with the director Simon Langton. A week later he delivered a brilliant script and we subsequently got an audience of thirteen million for our first episode.

Another reluctant deliverer of completed scripts was dear Johnnie Byrne, creator of such series as *All Creatures Great and Small* and *Heartbeat*, who wrote the opening episodes of a series on a country vet I produced called *Noah's Ark*. Johnnie was always on the lookout for valid-sounding excuses for missed deadlines. 'The dog ate it' was a good standby in the old days until his dog died, presumably of print poisoning; once he was computer literate, there were more crashes of his computer than there were on the M25. He was the only man I've ever met to have three grandmothers die. He admitted that he loved the idea of writing scripts but didn't actually enjoy writing them. He would think of any possible reason why he couldn't sit at his desk and write. Sick cats had to be taken to the vet, elderly relatives visited, doctor's appointments kept, children taken to and from school, accountants and bank managers met, the list was endless.

'Greg thinks there are far too many of your clients, friends, family and even employees appearing in your shows,' Nick Elliott announced to me during a game of croquet on the lawn of his country estate in Dorset, bought with the help of a generous tranche of shares handed to him when LWT won the London franchise.

This was a little unfair, as the clients who worked on my shows were usually high-profile actors who had had their arms twisted by me to appear, as our rates were not overly generous. Friends were unpaid and thrilled just to be there. Robert Pattinson and his parents were very excited to be the winning bid in a fundraising auction that offered them the opportunity to take part in *Noah's Ark* as extras. They were less excited when they finally saw the show several months later. After a long day's filming, their appearance had been reduced to a fleeting glimpse in a very wide long shot for a couple of seconds. Hardly value for money, though Robert did make up for it later.

My accountant spent a very pleasant afternoon sitting in the waiting room of the veterinary practice with his dog, as did my doctor and a teacher from Molly's school who, by a happy coincidence, was holidaying in the area. My father- and mother-in-law managed to avail themselves of the lunchtime catering facilities ahead of the cast and crew. In a later episode of *Noah's Ark*, Jack featured as a young boy with a sick rabbit and, in an attempt to ingratiate himself with me, the director gave Jack a line of dialogue. Sadly, when his time came to deliver it, Jack developed a major speech impediment and had to have several runs at it before he became audible. Nick suggested that we should re-voice him, but I drew the line at that. I did, however, agree to have his teeth fixed, which cost me a fortune, as Hilary insisted we use the royal orthodontist Alan Lynch.

Things got to a critical level in 1988 when we found the family house of our dreams, 10 Lower Common South on Putney Common. There was, however, a small problem: in order to buy it, not only did we have to sell our Hammersmith house but also our cottage in Kent. Fortunately the seller of the Putney house wanted a delayed completion, which gave us six months to shift both of ours, so we exchanged contracts and put them on the market. It was at this point that the housing market had one of its dramatic crashes; I now found myself having bought at the top of a very buoyant market, trying to sell in a very depressed and dying one.

And there was a welcoming 18 per cent bridging loan waiting for me at the end. To add to my worries, Hilary was pregnant with Molly and I was in the process of being taken to court by an ex-girlfriend.

We were one month away from completion when I decided to ring the estate agent and put the wind up him.

'You've got to be more aggressive, Howard,' I told Mr Cundey, the agent who was handling the sale. 'That's what estate agents are supposed to be: *aggressive*.'

Unfortunately, he took my instructions too literally and told our only potential buyer, Mr Stoat, who couldn't make his mind up about whether he did or didn't want the garage included in the sale, to 'shit or get off the pot!' This, I felt, was a touch extreme, as Mr Stoat, a very gentle, middle-aged insurance broker from Edenbridge, didn't look like a man who would be forced into making a decision by that kind of language. But to my surprise, it did the trick, and Stoat stayed 'on the pot' and duly obliged to the extent of a cash offer for the asking price.

On our other house, progress was virtually non-existent. It had been on the market with various hopeless agents and we were beginning to get desperate. The barrel was scraped when a young Asian couple, who could hardly speak English, told me that they were really looking for a house with a large garden and a swimming pool. So why were they looking in Hammersmith, I wondered? And then, one morning, dangerously close to the end of February, I got a call from a very hooray young man at Marsh and Parsons telling me that he had a Mrs Lizzy Crawford who would like to have a look at the house.

To describe the welcome she received from us as warm would be wholly inadequate. Forget the red carpet, this was the golden carpet, complete with choir and angels. Tea, sandwiches, walnut layer-cake on a cake stand; Hilary even baked some bread to give the kitchen a welcoming aroma and there were so many flowers in our bedroom, it looked like a chapel of rest. Mrs Crawford loved it. She told us that she had just gone through a messy divorce; the money had been sorted and she was now wanting to move fast but needed to see a couple of other houses before making a decision. Two days passed before Hooray Henry rang and said that Mrs Crawford would like to come and look at the house again.

It was at this juncture that desperation pointed me in the direction of Nigel Havers. I had an idea that was devious, deceitful and unprincipled. Even I paused for a moment – not a very long moment, but a pause nonetheless – before setting it in train. I explained the problem to Nigel and he immediately agreed to my plan. He was a friend and, although he thought it was pretty shitty too, he realised that these were desperate times.

As Lizzie was munching into her second cucumber sandwich, the doorbell rang. It was Nigel dropping by for an early drink.

'May I introduce Lizzie Crawford?' I said.

Nigel took a chocolate éclair off the cake stand and gave her a beaming smile.

'Haven't we met before?' he asked. 'Or if we haven't, why haven't we?' he oozed.

'No, I don't think so, but I certainly know you. I've so enjoyed watching you in *The Charmer*. What are you up to at the moment?'

'Well, not a lot currently. I'm moving house at the moment. Where do you live, Lizzie?

'Well, maybe here,' she gushed. 'I'm thinking of buying this house.'

Nigel then told her, over a glass of champagne, which Hilary had produced, what a wonderful area it was and how he had always regretted moving away. It was only because his soon-to-be-ex-wife had wanted more space that they had moved south of the river.

'But I'd love to get back here . . . I have my eye on a house up the road,' he said. 'It would be great to have you as a neighbour.'

After another glass of champagne, Nigel headed for the front door.

'I know how tough it is moving on after a divorce,' he said. 'I do hope we will meet again; at least I'll know where you are,' he added with a wink, before he gave her a kiss on her forcibly proffered cheek.

Nigel had, of course, slightly massaged the truth about his divorce. It had been over a year and he had already moved on.

'Charmer by name, charmer by nature,' she said after he'd left. 'And what an amazing coincidence that he might be living up the road.'

'Yes, isn't it a small world?' I said.

The sale went through. We didn't need the bridging loan; we moved to Putney and lived there happily ever after. In the end, Nigel didn't buy the house up the road, but he could well have done had his new wife not wanted to live in the country.

10

Godparenting

As I was born in April 1940, I think the last thing on my parents' minds were godparents. The British Expeditionary Force was being driven back to the coast of France by the Nazis, ending up in Dunkirk, and the Blitz on London would reach its full force three months later. My father was in the RAF with his friend Alan, whom he had sounded out for godfatherly duties, but sadly Alan was killed a few weeks later. My other godfather-to-be, Peter Roberts, never got off the Dunkirk beaches. Nora had thought of asking Auntie Betty to become my godmother but both sisters were too traumatised to think about such trivial things. So I have spent my whole life being un-godparented, thanks to those beastly Germans.

I was determined that my children would not only have godparents but plenty of them. To my mind, the perfect godparent is very rich, a single person of the unmarrying kind, who preferably has no siblings or close relatives, no other godchildren, and is quite elderly and not in the best of health. I didn't follow any of these criteria. Selection is a nightmare. Actors, generally speaking, are hopeless. My children had six of them and over the years lost three; a 50 per cent drop-out rate. One of Jack's left me as a client, only to return eight years later. Jack suspected that this had nothing to do with our professional relationship; it was just a ruse to avoid the heavy present-giving years between the ages of ten and eighteen. And one never mentioned Barney's name again after the christening service, although he did call his new puppy after him. So Barney found himself godfather-light and Hugh Massingberd generously offered to make up the numbers and be his honorary godfather. He couldn't have made a better job of it. Hugh was a true polymath and a serial stage door stalker, which is how we met, when my client Moray Watson played James Lees-Milne in Hugh's play *Ancestral Voices*, and we subsequently became close friends.

Hugh had a huge influence on Barney, who absolutely adored him. They shared two major areas of interest: cricket and eating. When he was eleven, Hugh would regularly take him to Lord's and the Oval; and whenever Barney returned from these outings, most of his reportage, apart from the cricket, would be about the amazing restaurant Hugh had taken him to before the game, and where he had introduced Barney to the joys of lobster or grouse.

'Grouse is all about the trimmings,' he told Barney. 'Game chips, streaky bacon, redcurrant jelly, gravy and lashings of bread sauce.'

'Hugh had two extra portions of bread sauce,' Barney told us.

'But watch out for the shot,' said Hugh, 'I don't want your parents saddled with a vast dental bill for a broken tooth.'

As if that wasn't enough, Hugh would always have prepared a hamper for the tea interval: sandwiches, scotch eggs, pork pies, fruit cake, tea, ginger beer, all for the two of them. I often wondered how he managed to carry it all. There would always be a visit to the MCC shop and Barney would return weighed down with merchandise: hats, caps, umbrellas, stationery and various containers full of sweets and chocolates.

Barney rang me once from a restaurant near the Oval.

'Daddy, do you know what we had for lunch?'

'No, what? Roast ptarmigan?' I said.

'No, haggis with a poached egg. It was delicious. Hugh had two poached eggs.'

The first time I lunched with Hugh, he invited me to join him at The Kensington Place, then run by his great friend Rowley Leigh. Ten minutes late, I walked past the windows of the restaurant, where I saw Hugh already eating. I thought this surprising, as Hugh was a stickler for good manners. Why would he have started without me? When I reached the table, he pushed the food away, offering me a flustered apology.

'I'm really sorry, Michael. Rowley insisted that I had this whilst I was waiting.'

'Not a bit,' I said, 'what is it?'

'Well, to be honest, it's one of my favourites on his breakfast menu. I did have breakfast this morning but he said that the smoked haddock was sublime today, so I had some with a poached egg on top. Don't worry, I've still got plenty of room left for lunch.'

And he had.

Hugh also took me to various clubs he was a member of, including The Oriental in Stratford Place, which, he said, served the best curry in London. That was going to be a bit of a challenge for me, not being a lover of Asian food. But I needn't have worried, Hugh had rung ahead, and when his lamb rogan josh arrived, a delicious sirloin steak arrived for me, accompanied by a half-bottle of Château La Lagune 1982. Hugh by then had given up drinking, but he certainly knew his way around a wine list.

Barney was also very lucky to have one of Hugh's favourite actresses as his godmother, Angela Thorne. I first met Angela when she was playing Penelope Keith's best friend Marjorie in the TV series *To the Manor Born,* which also featured my urbane client Peter Bowles. I became Angela's agent shortly thereafter. Amongst other things, Angela was the best Margaret Thatcher of them all, playing her in John Wells's stage play, *Anyone for Denis?* A mother of two sons herself – one of whom is the actor Rupert Penry-Jones – she knew all about boys. She and her husband Peter used to take Barney to the National Theatre every Christmas and, like Hugh, she always talked to him as though he was an adult rather than a child. Incredibly generous, she made Barney feel special, and trips out with Angela were always a treat.

My youngest son shares many traits with me, to the extent that Hilary claims we are clones. One particular trait is our love of a fad. We will both become obsessed with collecting certain things, sometimes for only a few weeks, sometimes for many months, before the obsession subsides.

Angela was always very happy to indulge Barney's latest fad, although she did draw the line on one occasion, when she had come over to take him out for his birthday.

'I haven't bought you a present yet, Barney,' she said as she finished her tea in our kitchen, 'I don't know what the latest must-have item is for you boys at the moment.'

Barney's craze at the time was American comics, and he had put together a modest collection. A shop called 30th Century Comics, near our house, dealt mainly in rare or limited-edition comics for the discerning collector, and Barney often gave it admiring glances whenever we passed the shop.

'Well,' said Barney, 'there are a few comics I've got my eye on in 30th Century Comics, so I wonder if we might be able to go there and have a look?'

'Of course,' said Angela, 'what a splendid idea.'

And off they went.

When they returned, Barney rushed into the house carrying a very full carrier bag.

'Angela's bought me some really cool comics, Daddy,' said Barney.

He trotted off to his bedroom so that he could lay them out on the floor. Angela seemed a little muted.

'Did Barney behave himself?' I said.

'Oh, yes of course, Michael. He's such a lovely polite boy; you never need worry on that score. But I must confess it was a bit embarrassing in the shop, as I had told Barney he could have anything he wanted, so he made straight for the collectors area and picked out two or three comics that he was so excited to have found. Unfortunately the ones he chose were all upwards of sixty pounds each. I had no idea that a comic could be that expensive. He seemed very disappointed when I suggested that these were perhaps a little too expensive and would he mind picking something out of the normal racks. I don't want to seem mean, but I did feel that sixty pounds was a bit steep for a comic, even a collector's item. I just felt it was too much to spend, especially at his age [it was his seventh birthday], but maybe I am being mean? I hope I haven't ruined his birthday treat. What do you think, Michael?'

Poor Angela, she had obviously got herself into a real state about it all.

When we later took Hugh and Barney to the National Theatre to a matinee of *The Reporter*, in which Angela was playing the author Rosamond Lehmann, with tea backstage afterwards, we didn't know at the time that it was to be one of our last outings with Hugh.

Hugh spent his last weeks in a hospice in Kensington. His ever-loving but mildly eccentric wife Ripples had a large collection of soft toys, some of which she brought into the hospice so that Hugh wouldn't be lonely when she wasn't there. A particular favourite of theirs was Panda, which became a useful distraction during a dreadful time. One day, as we were leaving the hospice, having seen Hugh for what turned out to be the last time, Ripples accompanied us to the front door. As we negotiated the long corridor, we saw a porter pushing what looked horribly like a dead body under a shroud towards us. Ripples, carrying Panda, immediately turned to face the wall.

'I didn't want him to see a dead body,' she said when the porter had passed. 'It would have upset him dreadfully.'

Of course it wasn't a dead body, but it was sweet that she thought it might be, and that Panda shouldn't see it. She loved Hugh so much, as did we all.

Jack was very fortunate to have one of the all-time best godparents in Richard Griffiths. Richard wrote many wonderful letters to Jack from the day he was born until he turned eighteen. When Richard died in 2013, Jack delivered the following eulogy at his memorial service at St James's Piccadilly.

Good afternoon. I am here to talk to you today as Richard's godson. Having spoken to his other godchildren I think I speak on their behalf when I say that we were truly blessed to have the most incredible godfather imaginable, who enhanced and enriched our lives beyond measure.

I'm also going to apologise in advance, as I've never been asked to speak at a memorial before, if I start blubbing during this. I may be a 25-year-old adult male but at the best of times I have the emotional constitution of a heavily hormonal pregnant woman. Indeed the other day I found myself crying uncontrollably at an episode of *Deal Or No Deal*, so God knows how I'm going to get through this in one piece.

I was fortunate to have Richard in my life on account of my father, who was Richard's agent for twenty-five years. My father always used to tell me he resented actors, as they took 90 per cent of his earnings. But it was fitting that when my father retired, Richard was the final client on his books, and even once they parted ways, they remained the closest of friends.

Upon being invited to be my godfather twenty-five years ago, Richard was pragmatic about the appointment and was keen to make sure his talents were best exploited.

'I'd better take care of the boy's moral compass,' he told my father over the phone. A very specific statement, but a sentiment that makes more sense when I tell you that he'd just been informed that my other godfather was going to be Nigel Havers.

Throughout my life Richard was always there for me. He'd be there at my birthdays, let me come and visit him on the set and introduce me to his fellow cast members, like I was the most important person in the world. Encouraging me in our shared love of drawing. But perhaps most significantly, he would call me up when I was down in the dumps, having failed to get into the school play, to inform me that in his humblest of opinions, the director of said play was 'a talentless arse.'

Looking back on this, it's depressing how many times he had to make that call.

But most memorably, Richard would write to me, the most incredible handwritten illustrated letters, packed with anecdotes, whimsical fairy tales, salacious showbiz gossip and bizarre tangents and flights of fancy, that when they were read to me as a child would leave me wide-eyed in amazement, as well as hugely entertaining my parents. I am so lucky that in this digital age of emails, texts and what my father refers to as 'the twatbook', I have this treasure trove of memories that I will always be able to cherish.

And when Heather asked me to speak to you today, I felt compelled to revisit these cherished letters, to read you some of his words to me and in doing so reveal the side of Richard that I knew and loved.

The letter I'm going to share with you was written to me on my third birthday. It was eleven pages long, so you will appreciate that this is a slightly abridged version.

My Dear Old Jack,

Firstly, let me congratulate you on your latest and currently most spectacular achievement of reaching your third birthday, well done. I will return to this most giddy of subjects in a moment but Firstly I should like to apologise for not making your birthday party, I was otherwise engaged and thus missed out on the event and all the floozies who I hear were in attendance.

I am currently writing to you 'as from' my glamorous West End dressing room whereas, in reality, I am in my bedroom in the flat, in Henrietta Strasse, Covent Garden, at the top of 3 million, four hundred and ninety-seven thousand and 21 steps. This is the kind of magic you can employ when those you are writing to, cannot actually see you when you are doing the writing. This is important stuff for your future reference. This helps you off all kinds of tricky hooks, so don't forget.

I think you ought to see my show at the Almeida Theatre but I don't think 'your people' would be too thrilled about it. There is a little local difficulty, which your poor old dad is too polite to describe in detail but I think I know what it is. It happens at the end of the first half of the show (the play by the way will be a legendary production of Luigi Pirandello's *The Rules of The Game*).

The little local difficulty to which I refer is Nicola Pagett's small but perfectly formed left breast, which is daringly pointed at the audience for 11 seconds. He was his usual coy self about it, your dad that is, but I could tell that he felt distinctly iffy about the possibility that upon seeing this inflammatory piece of nature's majesty, you might unthinkingly rush out and clamp your lips upon it in fond memory of days gone by.

Naturally were you to do so, it would have a radical impact upon the whole show. You will notice however I use the word 'radical'. I do not, necessarily, use the word 'disastrous'.

I'd like to return to my first paragraph. What you may ask was so very spectacular about reaching your third birthday, when everyone who is older has already done it, and when even your sister Molly is going to do it in the next couple of Novembers? Well, I'll tell you; you have done something which is mathematically extraordinary. Do you realize that in the past 12 months you have increased your age by 50 per cent? Well you have.

I should advise you, however, that if you are wise, and why shouldn't you be, you are best not to do it again. You see according to my calculations, if you keep on with this business of increasing your age by 50 per cent each year, it means that in the year 2006 – when you should be 18 and scouting around the place for a university some-where, you will in fact be one thousand, three hundred and thirteen years, eight months, four days, four hours and forty-eight minutes old. And I for one, who will by then be pushing 60, doubt if you would be recognisable as old JPBW. So please don't do it again. Mind you, there are some pretty weird birds in the Old Testament who came somewhere between Adam and Noah who prob-ably indulged in this 50 per cent lark. I have my doubts about Methuselah for one.

I am writing this page in a pretty hot pink because it is basically all about females and sex.

As you know we have two cats. The more glamorous of the two is a lilac pointed Siamese called Dippy, which is short for Serendipity but also because she is very stupid. The other cat is younger, with a more strokable fur, and she is of a breed known as the Burmese Blue. This second cat is called Dulcie because she is grey. There once was a famous actress called Dulcie Gray, but that has nothing to do with anything.

Dulcie, who is not quite as old as Molly, is going to have some kittens. As I'm sure you can imagine the Neighbourhood is pretty scandalised by this under-age bonking business. I mean what would your neighbours say if young Molly [then aged two] suddenly produced a couple of Kittens, see what I mean?

Now you have the advantage of me here, because I wish to talk about these rumours I hear about you tearing around with a rather fast, not to say risqué, crowd which hangs around the Haymarket, St James's and all too often Putney Common. And as any fool can see from 20 paces you are far too deeply for my liking, in the red. The advantage you have is that only you and your sainted mother know the true state and extent of both your accounts and your gambling debts and I don't. So, having put you in the picture, I am now going to put you in the black. I am going to pin your pocket money to £1.33 per week and I will adjust it upwards or downwards at Christmas. Enclosed, please find my cheque for £69.16 and don't breathe a word to ANYONE about it.

I dread to think what your poor old pops would make of all these fast women and slow horses, which we have managed, by the skin on the custard, to keep out of the tabloid nasties.

And what pray, were you looking for exactly in Shepherd's Market last Tuesday? No, don't answer, we will never raise that topic again. Just remember whenever you are tempted by the world's nefarious delinquencies, there is always someone on a number 16 bus – that will see you and talk about you the very next chat that they have.

In closing I want to give you an important word of advice – Don't. If in any doubt, just Don't. Ok?

On the other hand, if you fancy your chances, and you're pretty sure that nobody can see you anyway, Do it.

However, just remember this, There are Godfathers, few in numbers, but they're to be found if searched for, who, when their advice is not followed and disaster ensues, will Not say, 'I told you so.' I am not one of these.

Ciao Caro (That's Italian)

Riccardo xxxx

And remember, I was only three!

So in the words of my dear old Riccardo, 'Do it.'

Whether it be bringing out a bottle of champagne when in the company of great friends, telling that extra story even though you were meant to be somewhere five minutes ago, or taking the time to write an eleven-page letter to your three-year-old godson. Do it.

If we can live our lives as fully as Richard did, with even a fraction of the kindness, intelligence, wit, charm and generosity that he possessed, we will be better people for it and we will make the world a richer and funnier place.

Ciao caro!

Shortly after Richard died, Jack wrote an 'In Memorium' piece for the *Daily Telegraph,* which included the following.

From the day I was born, 'Uncle Richard', as he was known to me, Uncle Monty and Uncle Vernon to the rest of the world, took an incredible interest in my develop-ment. He seemed intent on making sure I turned out to be a well-rounded and -informed young man and clearly felt a great sense of responsibility.

Where some godparents will give you a box of orna-mental spoons at the christening then conveniently forget about your existence and totally shirk any duty (not mentioning any names – she knows who she is), Richard threw himself into the godfather role, as he did with every role he took on, with great gusto. It was my father, his agent for twenty-five years, who asked him to take the part; it was one he absolutely nailed.

No matter where he was working, home or abroad, he would always make a point of writing to me. The most remarkable thing about this correspondence was that the letters were written for an adult reader rather than a child. The first one, written after my christening, referred to the service, the 'peculiar' vicar my parents had chosen and how impressive the guest list was. It ended with a detailed paragraph about how good the wine had been and who'd drunk too much of it (namely my dad).

Over the next few years, topics covered included the Doges of Venice, the behaviour of his wife Heather's new cat and his doubts as to whether the Labour Party's election victory of 1997 was indeed 'A New Dawn', something I was fairly ambivalent about, being only eight at the time.

On my second birthday, Richard wrote to me about the necessity of having some financial back-up in the form of a running-away fund. He had attempted to run away himself on several occasions but had never pulled it off, due to lack of funds. Every subsequent year Richard would send me a cheque on my birthday to be added to the fund, which he said could be used as soon as I met the right woman and wanted to up sticks.

Throughout my life, Richard managed to engage me with topics suitable for the age I had reached and fire up my enthusiasm for them. When I was four it was Robin Hood; he gave me intimate details of Robin's mode of dress, something that inspired me to want to wear nothing but green tights for the next six years. At five, it was the world of Horatio Hornblower, someone he loved and had an encyclopaedic knowledge of. He even came and talked to the boys at my school about the subject. 'Your godfather's coming to talk about a book?' said one of my friends to me, sceptically.

An hour later they were sitting totally captivated by him, begging for an encore. I always felt sorry for the poor man that had to follow Richard on stage and give a rather dreary talk about the history of the steam engine.

He even acted as my counsellor when things weren't going so well. When I failed to impress my teachers with my acting prowess, he would encourage me to carry on regardless. 'What do they know?' he said.

Going to see Richard in the theatre was always a delight. Apart from the thrill of seeing an actor who has delivered some of my favourite performances on the stage (in *The History Boys*, for example), there was the added excitement of going to see him afterwards. He'd always have a bottle of champagne in the fridge and even if the curtain had come down the performance would not be over as I and whoever else had been lucky enough to be invited backstage would be treated to our very own private performance. Anecdotes, stories about the theatre – even after an exhausting performance he was happy to entertain. He was the best story-teller I have ever met.

This is why I always loved Richard so much: as a child one appreciates the adults you meet who talk to you as if you are one of them, who don't patronise or look down their nose at you. When you were with Richard you always felt you were his equal.

I have only been an actor for a short time, but it is safe to say it's a profession that attracts the odd ego. But you could not meet a more humble man than Richard. In his presence everyone was the same. I remember the first time I met Daniel Radcliffe at the premiere of the first *Harry Potter*, in which Richard played the revolting Vernon Dursley. It was early in Daniel's career and he was quite shy and nervous and when I was introduced to him, I was pretty nervous too to be meeting Harry Potter. Richard instantly put us at ease: 'Daniel, this is my godson Jack, now if you haven't got a girlfriend you must meet Jack's sister Molly. She's beautiful.' Even on one of the biggest nights of his career he was able to diffuse any nerves with a bit of friendly matchmaking. Molly and Daniel, alas, never did meet.

I remember something my dad said one evening after a particularly galling conversation with an actor whose ego had got way out of control. 'If only they were all like Richard,' he said.

If only they were. I am so fortunate to have had this inspirational man in my life. How I will miss him.

11

On the Circuit

Unsurprisingly, I'd never heard of the Comedy Festival in Hereford, a county better known for its cattle than its comedy, and when asked in 2015 if I would like to be part of it, I immediately rang Neil. Neil Stacy, Doctor of Philosophy, medieval historian, distinguished actor and one of my oldest friends. The go-to man for me, when an unbiased opinion is needed pronto.

'I wouldn't go near it if I were you. You'd be mad. It's one thing telling amusing stories round a dinner table, quite another standing on a stage on your own for an hour and half making people laugh. You're not a comedian, Michael, only the father of one. Also it would take ages to get there; it's practically Wales and you know your feelings about the Welsh.' He had a point, so I swiftly declined.

I borrowed Neil's line when I called the promoter back.

'I'm not a comedian, just the father of one,' seemed a good answer I thought. The promoter was not going to leave it there, and waffled on about how much they loved me in *Backchat*, how they *really* wanted me and what a perfect balance I would be with Jack Dee who had already been booked. His flattery chipped away at my resolve and I found myself saying, 'Let me think it over.'

I was in danger of backing into the spotlight even further although it was at least in six months' time. A couple of days later I had lunch at the Wolseley, having rung to book a last-minute table. I was reminded of an agent friend who had done the same thing, with a less successful outcome. He had rung one evening and asked for a table in half an hour.

'I'm sorry, we're fully booked,' said the manager.

'But surely you keep a few tables for celebrities?' he said.

'Yes of course we do,' he replied. 'Who are you bringing?'

As I arrived at my table, I asked my friend Jeremy King, the world's greatest restaurateur, for his advice about my dilemma.

'Obviously it's up to you, but I've always thought that if you don't want to do something now, you're not going to want to do it any more in six months' time,' he told me sagely.

I can only say in mitigation that I must have been temporarily blinded by the spotlight because, inexplicably, I found myself ignoring both Neil and Jeremy's advice and saying 'yes' a couple of weeks later, having been wined and dined by the promoter. It's amazing what a good lunch and a nice bottle of wine can do to change one's mind after it's been firmly made up in the opposite direction.

A few months before I was due to make my stage debut at The Courtyard Theatre, Hilary happened to be in the area at the wedding of her goddaughter. She was travelling solo, as I generally speaking don't do weddings any more, especially as they now seem to go on for days. She thought she'd drop by the theatre to see how the bookings were going. Things didn't get off to a good start when the girl at the box office said that she'd never heard of me and had Hilary got the right theatre?

'He's part of the Comedy Festival,' said Hilary.

'What's his name again? Whitehead?' she said as she clicked away at her computer. This did not bode well.

'Whitehall. Michael Whitehall,' replied Hilary irritably.

'Ah, here it is. Oh I remember, Jack Dee is on the Saturday night and sold out in twenty-four hours. Now, let's see how Michael is doing on the Sunday.'

There was a pause.

'Twenty-six,' said the girl.

'What? There are only twenty-six tickets left?' asked Hilary.

'No, we've only sold twenty-six tickets, love. I think that's probably why I didn't recognise his name.'

'How many does it seat?'

'Four hundred and sixty, so he's got a wee way to go yet,' she added helpfully.

Hilary ploughed on.

'That's a bit of an understatement. That isn't even two rows! I don't see any advertising for it, does anyone actually know it's on?'

'Oh, we won't get the posters up until nearer the time. People round here don't seem to buy tickets too far in advance.'

'Unless they're Jack Dee fans, presumably.'

'But it's on the website, and I think you'll find there will be a lot of walk-in trade on the night.'

As the theatre wasn't in walking distance of anywhere, that seemed highly unlikely.

'There's going to need to be. I can't help thinking the odd poster in the foyer might help,' Hilary suggested as she set off for the station.

Hilary picked her moment to deliver the news to me. Given that I didn't want to do the show in the first place, this was not what I wanted to hear. I called the promoter and let rip about what a terrible idea the whole thing had been and how could he have thought that it was ever going to work? He tried to calm me down with talk of last-minute sales and the provinces coming 'out on the night', none of which was very believable given the location of the theatre on the fringes of sleepy Hereford. This was going to be a disaster.

'You've stuck me in some ghastly backwater. Hereford is hardly a throbbing metropolis. The Edinburgh Festival it ain't. And Hilary tells me that the theatre is on the outskirts of town, next to an industrial estate, so hardly prime "passing trade" territory.'

'Give it time, the theatre-going public of Hereford might surprise you,' he said unconvincingly.

A week before the show, Jack was having dinner at home and, as he played on the PS4 with his brother Barney, I called the promoter for an update. It was not good news; I struggled to keep my temper, a struggle that I invariably lose, as I told him I was going to have to pull out.

'What was all that about?' asked Jack.

'This ridiculous Comedy Festival in Hereford. I agreed to it months ago and now that it's a week away, they have only sold forty-eight tickets out of 460, and most of those are as a result of your mother begging her goddaughter and family to get their mates to buy tickets. It's so embarrassing. I can't believe I was talked into doing it by that dick of a promoter!' Forty-eight seats was still only a tenth of the capacity.

'When is it?' asked Jack.

'Next Sunday,' I replied.

'Why don't I come and do it with you? I'm busy for the next few weeks but I have Sunday night off. Mums could drive us up there and back. Molly and Barney could come too and fill two more seats,' he added.

'Are you absolutely sure?'

'Yeah, it'll be fun.'

The following day I delivered the news to the theatre, seeing as I didn't want the promoter getting the credit for the inevitable turnaround in sales when Jack was announced. Besides, he wasn't answering my calls as he presumably thought I was going to shout at him again. They duly announced Jack was going to do the show with me and it sold out within hours. I vowed never to do anything like that ever again. I'd had my head turned and it should now be turned firmly back in the other direction, where it had been very happily for most of my life, and I should retreat back out of the spotlight. Oh, and I should listen to Neil in future.

'It's just twenty minutes. It's a fun event and there is a fee. Henry Kissinger did it once and everyone on the committee thinks you would be brilliant,' said Tim Rice at the other end of the phone eighteen months later.

'I don't do speaking jobs, Tim; they're just not my thing. And I had a horror story on my last outing, so thanks so much, but no thanks.'

As I got up at the Saints and Sinners Christmas Lunch at The Savoy Hotel, having been introduced as the celebrity guest speaker by a red, frock-coated master of ceremonies, I realised that I had made a terrible mistake … yet again. The hundred or so male guests continued to chat to one another and there seemed to be a lot of comings and goings, mainly goings, at the back of the cavernous ballroom we were in. I had misheard Tim, who had not asked for twenty minutes but ten. As I was struggling with a long anecdote about Elaine Stritch, my audience by now having metaphorically disappeared, the master of ceremonies slipped a note in front of me written on the back of a menu. It read 'I'm sorry, sir, but you need to end NOW.'

As I blushingly walked towards the exit, conscious of hostile eyes following me across the room, a very drunk man, who had the look of Tommy Trinder about him, swayed over to me.

'If you do something like that again, old boy,' he said, 'I'd get your son to give you better jokes.'

Henry Kissinger once said that the great thing about being a celebrity is that, if you bore people, they think it's their fault. Clearly not at the Saints and Sinners Christmas Lunch.

As I came out of the back entrance of the hotel, a van driver opened his window and shouted 'S'cuse me mate. Ain't you the actor who plays Jack Whitehall's dad?' 'No I'm not actually,' I replied curtly. As he drove off, he shouted, 'I bet you wish you were!'

* * *

Hilary helps me with my emails, which is incredibly kind of her, as I am a complete Luddite when it comes to technology. I am still very unreliable with a television remote control but can do a limited amount on my iPhone, but certainly not anything that requires attachments or other complicated things. So, she dips in and out of my email and very little gets past her. Unfortunately, it was she who first saw the invitation to be a guest speaker on a cruise ship that specialised in bespoke educational cruises. Had I seen it before her, I would certainly have consigned it to trash, but she got there first and before I could say Hereford Comedy Festival, she had picked out a cruise that included Bermuda, the Turks and Caicos, the Bahamas and, best of all, Cuba.

'This is the time to go,' she said. 'The Cubans are about to let the Americans back in and it will change beyond recognition. That's our cruise.' My heart sank; a weekend in Paris maybe, but Cuba? I called Neil.

'Hilary's gone completely mad, Michael,' he said.

'I know, I can't think of anything I would want to do less, but she's so excited, I thought I'd better just knuckle down and get on with it.'

'There are so many reasons why you shouldn't,' said Neil. 'Firstly you'll be stuck on a bloody cruise ship with a lot of ghastly people with shaven heads and tattoos and secondly, OK, they'll be a captive audience, but you'll be a captive audience too because you won't be able to get off the damn thing. I repeat, Michael, won't be able to get off. And . . . you can't swim!'

A month before we left, President Obama announced that he was going to be the first US president to visit the country since 1928 and, as luck would have it, his visit coincided with our three days in Havana.

'What are the chances of that?' Hilary said. 'Probably find we won't even be allowed to get off the ship.' Perhaps the whole thing will be cancelled, I thought to myself. No such luck.

My ten days on the high seas were all that Neil had predicted. The guest speaker accommodation was wholly inadequate (a very pokey cabin, with one port-hole, opposite the passenger laundrette), so at vast expense I upgraded us to a cabin that at least had a bath in it. I don't do showers.

Even when we hit dry land, there were endless problems. Cuba was in lockdown, preventing us getting near to any of the historic monuments and sights, but even worse was being constantly kettled into side streets for hours, due to the presidential motorcade. We had to skirt past the Bahamas altogether, as Grand Inagua had had a load of sand dumped into the harbour by a passing hurricane, making it inoperable for cruise ships. The Turks and Caicos 'shutting for Easter', just as the ship docked there, meant that there was no way of buying anything, apart from a selection of ghastly sun hats and baseball caps. And then we reached Bermuda, from where we made our escape home.

I did my best to make the most of it – well, up to a point. As a guest speaker I was expected to host dinners in the evenings, a job that I left Hilary to sort out. We had mixed results with these – mostly grim; some, I would have to grudgingly admit, quite entertaining. A retired SAS general and his wife from Hereford (where were they for the Hereford Comedy Festival when I needed them?) who were charming, and a very jolly red-faced character from Belfast and his wife, who lived in Bath and were at least capable of intelligent conversation and cruise-based banter. Less engaging was a retired chartered accountant from Dorking, who seemed to have only one tooth in working order and I had to make him repeat everything he said to me before I understood a word, though in most cases it wasn't worth the effort. And a very dull photographer from Warwick, who insisted on sharing her work from the cruise with us, which – given that we were at sea for most of the time – was stultifyingly boring. There are only so many ways of taking pictures of the sea and the sky.

But the main problem I had was that unless I was with Hilary, I never knew who anyone was or where I was. Finding one's way around a ship is not an easy thing, as I quickly discovered. Every corridor looked the same, and I never knew if I was heading forwards or backwards on the ship. I would wander around, sometimes for hours, trying to find my way back to our very expensive sun deck cabin. The only people I did actually manage to recognise were three ladies from Yorkshire, who had all left their husbands at home and were very good at leading me back to my cabin, often after a large Hendrick's and tonic. When I finally got back there, it was usually full of people, with whom Hilary had become lifelong friends. Several couples actually turned up as VIP guests at some of Jack's stand-up dates several months later.

The structure of the actual talks was wafer thin. Hilary would interview me and I would rattle off a bunch of well-worn anecdotes. After thirty years of marriage, it was quite weird having her ask me where I was born, where I had lived, how I became an agent and who my clients were, but Hilary is a fine actress and managed to make it work. At the end of the first show, the Entertainments Manager introduced himself to me and gave me a very lukewarm appraisal of my performance.

'Most of our speakers use slides for their lectures. Have you ever thought of doing that? It would make your talk more interesting.' As he moved away, I was approached by a lady who I assumed was a fan. It turned out that she was the actor Derek Nimmo's sister. I had told the following story about her brother during the show.

Derek may have made a career out of playing scatty clerics, but there was nothing scatty about him in reality. He ran a very profitable business producing plays on very tight budgets for expats in the Middle East. Ray Cooney was a favourite playwright of the English-speaking audiences of Dubai.

I first met Derek in Sydney, when he was producing and starring in a play called *Why Not Stay for Breakfast?* Over a light port, he asked me what kind of a deal I was on at the hotel. I wasn't quite sure what he meant and told him that as I was travelling on a publicity tour with my client Kenny More and my bill was being picked up by the film company.

'Do they pay for your laundry?' enquired Derek.

'Well I guess they do, but I'm flying on to Hong Kong tomorrow, so I haven't really got any.'

'Do you mind if I put some of my laundry on your bill before you go?'

I didn't quite know what to say; I hardly knew Derek and wasn't that keen on getting acquainted with his laundry.

'What time's your flight?'

The following morning, there was a knock at the door. It was the maid with a large basket of clothes.

'This is from Mr Nimmo.'

A few minutes later, there was another knock and another maid.

'I believe you have some laundry, sir.'

She removed the basket.

And when I came to pay the bill, there it all was under SUNDRIES.

Obviously I thought Nimmo's sister was going to be very annoyed at me having told this story, but in fact she had thoroughly enjoyed it and added, 'I wouldn't be at all surprised if he had had all the cast's laundry in there too.'

The second show was rather less well attended than the first, although I was pleased to see Derek Nimmo's sister had made a return visit. But I put that down to the choppy sea that night, although there was a rumour circulating around the ship that the commotion at the back of the theatre during the second half of our opening show had in fact been an elderly man; he had collapsed and died during the show and was being kept in a deep freeze until we reached the next port. Remarks such as 'The Whitehalls' show died a death' and 'Michael Whitehall managed to bore him to death,' etc., etc., were rife. I asked the Russian captain if he had any news on the gentleman's demise, but he didn't seem to know anything about it and – as he had very limited English – I decided not to pursue it further.

The three charming Yorkshire ladies, whom Hilary had named my 'fan club', were very taken with my story about Nora and the '*à la cartes*', which became quite a talking point among the passengers during the cruise. The ladies were delightful and they laughed at all my jokes. What more could I want?

Dyed hair works for women, seldom for men. Hairdressers will spin you the same line – 'a light rinse will make you look ten years younger'. It actually makes you look a lot older. What's wrong with grey or white hair? Just imagine how much better Paul McCartney, Robert Redford, Cliff Richard and Donald Trump (maybe not the latter) would look with normal hair.

I'm not a man who makes spontaneous decisions often, and particularly not regarding my hair, but with a TV appearance on the horizon, I decided to abandon my £10 barber's shop off Putney High Street and give a rather more upmarket establishment in the Fulham Road a shot. Andreas of Mayfair Hair Design was quite a long way from Mayfair, being at the wrong end of the Fulham Road, but it was newly opened and decked out with lots of chrome, moody lighting and shiny leather chairs, and something called a Gentleman's Spa in the basement. What went on down there I dreaded to think.

Andreas, his accent swerving around from French, to mid-Atlantic, and ending up in south London, was flamboyant. Not a tall man, he had given himself (or maybe his young assistant Paul had) a very bouffant hairstyle – it could almost have been a wig – that barely moved when he threw his head back, which he did almost continuously. He inspected my hair, lifting up strands of it and scrutinising them with what can only be described as derision.

'Who cut your hair?' he enquired.

'Pedro off Putney High Street,' I replied.

'They are not hairdressers. That man is a shearer!'

'Well I've been going to him for years and he is very sweet.'

'He may be sweet, but he's shorn you. Your hair has no style, no theme, no balance.' Andreas was getting carried away. It was eleven o'clock, I had a lunch date in Barnes at one and I needed a haircut. He looked at me via the enormous mirror hanging in front of us.

'Do you know what would really improve your look?' he asked in a slightly aggressive voice.

'Plastic surgery?' I ventured. I thought I would insert a little light humour into the proceedings. Missing the joke, he said, 'No, no! The look of your hair, silly.'

'Tell me,' I replied.

'A very light rinse.'

'No way. I do *not* want my hair dyed, thank you very much.' Andreas looked to be on the verge of tears. Pedro never got emotional about my hair.

'Mr Whitehall, I would *never* dye your hair. I would just apply a very light rinse to highlight the grey and complement your colouring. Distinguished, discreet, a

172

pepper-and-salt look. Think Cary Grant in *Charade* or George Clooney in *Solaris*.'

'Look, Andreas, I really don't have time for a George Clooney today. I'm already running late.'

'You'll be away in an hour, promise,' he said.

'And looking twenty years younger,' added Paul.

'Well, if it really is a very light rinse and if you think it will look good, then let's go for it,' I said, unable to put up with any more sales talk from him.

'Paul, take Mr Whitehall over to the basin,' he said to his assistant. I thought I heard Paul say, 'Cheers Fred,' but maybe I misheard him. Paul relieved me of my spectacles – I'm blind without them – and got to work.

Application of the light rinse, combing through, waiting, brushing, more washing; my hair had never had so much attention in its life. From time to time, Andreas (or Fred) would come and speak to me. Like a surgeon during an operation, he would assure me that all was going well and that he and Paul and indeed everyone else in the salon, including a rather surly looking girl sweeping up hair, were pleased with the progress.

'Tea or coffee?' asked the hair sweeper in a rather lispy whine.

'Not just at the moment, thank you,' I replied. I certainly didn't need any more activity around the porcelain basin my head was being held down in. Then after some cutting, more washing, conditioning, a fingertip massage, more combing, a final rinse, blow-drying and styling, Andreas whipped off my gown and proudly announced in yet another accent:

'*Finito!*'

He handed me back my spectacles.

I put them back on.

I looked in the mirror.

Looking back at me was a shell-shocked 71-year-old man with a pale orange wig sitting on top of his head.

'It looks wonderful,' shrieked Andreas.

'Marvellous,' said Paul.

'Really nice,' added the hair sweeper. It was a total and utter disaster.

'Let me show you the back,' said Andreas. Now I have never understood why hairdressers show you the back of your head. I have absolutely no interest in what the back of my head looks like. Perhaps I would if I'd asked Andreas to give me a Mohican, or if I was a member of the BNP and wanted a swastika shaved on to my head. Otherwise the back of my head is not an area I have ever had much interest in or any desire to have 'shown' to me after a haircut. However, on this occasion I thought it might be wise to let Andreas activate the proffered small hand-held mirror behind my head. The sight that greeted me was even worse than the front, as not only was the hair dark brown, but Andreas had given me what used to be referred to as a DA. (A 'Duck's Arse', for the uninitiated.) I peered back into the main mirror. I looked like Dirk Bogarde in *Death in Venice*. The dye will start dribbling down my face in a minute, I thought.

Paul returned with another offer of coffee.

'I'm absolutely fine, thank you Paul. I actually need to crack on to my lunch date. Can you bring me the bill please?' The bill arrived. Forty-five pounds for the cut and another £45 for 'extra services'.

'Excuse me,' I called over to Andreas. 'I pay Brian a tenner. This is ridiculous, and what is this sum for extra services?'

'That's for the rinse.'

'It sounds very dodgy, as though I was getting some other services in your Gentleman's Spa in the basement.'

'Of course not, Michael, but if you'd like to . . .' said Paul.

'No, that is not what I mean. If Mrs Whitehall saw "extra services" on the bill, she would certainly draw the wrong conclusion . . .'

As I was paying the bill, Andreas asked me if I would like a photograph of my hair.

'Whatever for?' I said.

'Well, you would have a record of the cut if you wanted to have it replicated in the future.' Was this man mad? It reminded me that when I had a colonoscopy a few years ago, my doctor had handed me a DVD of my procedure, 'just in case you want to show it to anyone,' he'd added. Of course I will, Doctor, I thought. I'll get some friends over for a drink one evening or maybe dinner, and then we can all sit around the TV afterwards with coffee and liqueurs and have a screening of the inside of my bowels. Ditto my rotator cuff surgery on my shoulder. And then throw in a few stills of my recent haircut at Andreas of Mayfair Hair Design.

Having declined a photographic record of Andreas's butchering of my hair, I paid my bill (no, I didn't want a copy for myself: showing Hilary that I had had £45 of extra services from a man called Andreas – or Fred – was not a good idea) and said goodbye to my new and soon-to-be-ex-hairdresser, with as much civility as I could muster.

I had half an hour before I was due to meet my lunch date Patricia Hodge, enough time to go home and re-inspect the horror that was my hair. It looked even worse than it had done in the shop. In ordinary daylight, without the help of the salon lights, it had gone from dark brown to jet black. My first thought was to cancel my lunch, but it was too late for that, Patricia would be on her way to the restaurant. I put on a Panama hat and, dreading the next couple of hours, headed off.

'You're looking very well,' said Patricia. 'Have you been away?'

I reminded her that going away was a rarity with me, but I had in fact had a week in Devon and the weather had been glorious.

'Well you're certainly still in holiday mode,' she replied. 'Are you planning to keep your hat on over lunch?'

We had been seated at a corner table in the restaurant, so it was quite dark.

'I think maybe I will,' I said. The waitress came over to take our order.

'Can I put your hat in the cloakroom for you?' she asked helpfully.

'No, I'm fine thanks.' We ordered.

Having mulled over it during the starters, I decided to bite the bullet and tell her about my earlier trip to Andreas's.

'I'm sure it's not that bad,' she said sweetly. 'You'll soon get used to it.'

'There is no way I will ever get used to it. The man is a total arsehole. How dare he make me look like a vain old man, trying to look young.'

'Michael, I'm sure you're overreacting. Take your hat off and let me see it.'

'No.'

'Go on, Michael, don't be ridiculous. I'm sure it's fine.'

'Okay.'

I removed my hat.

Patricia looked at me.

She paused.

'Does that mean that the carpet doesn't match the drapes?' she asked as she wiped away tears of laughter.

The following day I walked over to Pedro's barber's shop off Putney High Street.

'Blimey Michael, what's happened to you?'

'I don't want to talk about it, Pedro. I just want you to do something about it.'

'Not much I can do, Michael,' he said. 'But it'll grow out.'

'How long will that take?'

'A month maybe?'

'But I'm on *The Million Pound Drop* with Jack tomorrow night. What am I going to do?'

'I could cut it all off?'

'I can't go on looking like an elderly GI,' I protested.

'Well, you'll have to go on with it like that, and I'll sort you out next week.'

So, Davina McCall was confronted by the full pale orange horror story when I stepped off the stairs to take up my position before her on the set the following night. The only saving grace of the evening was that Jack and I managed to win a shed load of money for charity.

12

Into the Spotlight

I've long since come to the conclusion that agents are nothing but trouble. This of course still holds true, although that's really what they're there to be, and I thought that I'd probably been trouble for long enough. New pastures were required. When you're hot, you're hot and when you're not, you're not. But little did I know that a late and very unexpected career in front of the camera was about to unfold.

In 2010, Jack and his producer Ben Cavey asked if I would like to do an afternoon show with Jack at the Edinburgh Festival. Up to that point I had been in front of the camera only once. In the late 1990s, my friend the director Robert Young asked if I would like to play Jamie Lee Curtis's husband in a film he was directing called *Fierce Creatures*, which also starred John Cleese, Kevin Kline and Michael Palin. I politely declined. I was not a performer. I was the responsible businessman, not the creative, insane one. Well, Robert talked me into it, telling me how I would bring realism to the part, essentially playing myself, and what a joy it would be for me to hang out with Jamie and Kevin on set. I was duly sent the script and eagerly looked for the part of Mr Weston, the rich husband of the exotic Willa Weston. I found the scene; I found Mr Weston's appearance; I sadly found no dialogue. Robert had offered me a one-scene, non-speaking part. I'd been sold a pup; although I did get my day on set with Jamie and Kevin, including an extremely entertaining lunch with them both, and at least I was in the film.

Six months later, I went to the press preview in Leicester Square and sat next to Robert. As the lights went down, he whispered in my ear, 'I hope you enjoy it. Oh, and I forgot to say, sadly we had to cut your scene.' In fact the film wasn't the great success everyone had expected, maybe because I wasn't in it.

Back in Edinburgh, Ben and Jack said that they had come up with the concept of a talk show, with Jack interviewing performers who were up at the festival with shows to plug. I would join him on stage, sitting in a button-back leather chair looking grumpy. This was sounding suspiciously like another non-speaking role.

'Do you remember Madge in *The Dame Edna Experience*?' Ben said. 'We think you would be so funny.'

So, that was to be the shtick.

Jack was playing a week at the 1,200-seater EICC

with his solo stand-up show every night, and we were to do our live show in the Cabaret Bar at the Pleasance at four p.m. This was affectionately known as the 'Nicholas Parsons slot', as he had played this venue for the first three weeks of the festival for the last eleven years. After the first performance, where our guest was Simon Callow, who largely talked about the joys of corduroy trousers, to which I had chipped in liberally, a friend who lived in Edinburgh buttonholed me.

'Well done, old chap. You were Madge to Jack's Edna, only with a voice, weren't you?'

'I should have known that I wouldn't be able to shut you up,' said Jack.

By the end of our run at the Pleasance, we had had a sell-out crowd every afternoon, although it was only a 150-seater and it was teatime. A BBC commissioner, who had been reluctantly dragged along to see the show by his fifteen-year-old son, a fan of Jack's, decided to commission *Backchat* as a series for BBC3.

'This has legs,' he said. 'Every father and son in the land will relate to it. You in that button-back chair interrupting Jack's show . . . the format is perfect.'

Well, at least I'd finally got some lines.

One thing that helped to nail the commission was our appearance that autumn on the quiz show, *The Million Pound Drop*. The producer had seen us in Edinburgh and wanted to recruit us for a charity version of the show.

I had never heard of it and doubted that it would be my kind of thing. Wouldn't Jack like to do it with one of his comedy friends? No, he wanted to do it with me, and thought it would be a great idea if we nominated a local charity that Hilary volunteered for, Homestart in Richmond, and also various Alzheimer's charities, which sadly Hilary's father was in the grip of. Despite my alarming hair colour, which looked even worse under the television lights, it turned out to be a momentous evening for us both. We had expected to come away with £2,000 having lost the £1 million, but surpassed all expectations by winning £300,000. The charities were thrilled, Jack was thrilled; but I wasn't. I was still cursing myself for forgetting that Imelda Staunton hadn't won an Oscar for the film *Vera Drake*, otherwise we would have won £400,000.

It took several more live shows and a TV pilot of *Backchat* before we aired series one on BBC3 in 2013, followed by subsequent series and specials on BBC2. Because *Backchat* was pre-recorded several weeks before transmission, we weren't able to attract the hot US talent flying in to promote their latest film or play, so we had to work a lot harder to get guests; but we did manage to come up with some interesting pairings. I also discovered just how different people were to their onscreen personas. I had always found Jonathan Ross very resistible, but he turned out to be a charming man and very amusing. And Judy Murray was a revelation, and nothing like the severe lady in the Players' Box at Wimbledon. Two grand dames of the show-business world also turned out to be unexpectedly different from widely held perceptions. Joan Collins, according to people who knew her, would be very relaxed and very easy-going. Not the case. Although, in her defence, she had just flown in from LA, was jet-lagged and had never heard of Jack, me or the show. It begged the question: why had she agreed to do it? A question she clearly asked herself when she got up halfway through the recording and announced to Miranda Hart, her co-star on the sofa, and the studio audience, that she had to leave, as she had a dinner reservation. She was only enticed back on to the sofa with the offer of champagne, which a runner was dispatched to go and buy from the local corner shop.

The following week Cilla Black was booked to appear and the word on the street was that she could be difficult. In fact she was hugely endearing and, unlike Joan, had agreed to do the show because, as she told me in the makeup room beforehand, she was a huge fan of Jack. She told him during the show that, like us, she had recorded all her biggest hit television shows – *Blind Date* and *Surprise Surprise* – at ITV Studios, but in the *bigger* studio, she added with a beaming smile, just so that he knew his place. Sadly, it was to be her last TV appearance.

I was a little out of my depth with a few of the guests. Common ground was on the short side with Danny Dyer, somebody I had never heard of, but who Jack assured me was not only a big star but related to the royal family; then there was a charming young man called KSI, who politely asked me if I would perform with him, which I said I would be delighted to do. He then got completely out of control and continuously shouted 'Lamborghini' at me at the top of his voice, as did the strangely named Lethal Bizzle, who insisted on shouting 'Dench' at me throughout another show. I assumed it was because he must have known that I had been Dame Judi's agent many years ago, but it turned out that it was some sort of weird catchphrase of his. I later discovered that they were both rappers – a musical genre probably best avoided by the over-seventies. Mr Bizzle also introduced me to the Urban Dictionary, which I think he and Jack found more entertaining than I did. And what a delight Nick Hewer was, especially as I was sucking up to him in the hope of getting booked into 'Dictionary Corner' on *Countdown*. He kindly obliged. Jeremy Paxman was also good fun to have on the show and very different to his onscreen persona. When Gary Lineker, another guest, was reminded by Jack that he had shat himself in front of a worldwide audience during a televised World Cup game, swiftly followed by a discussion with his co-guests on the sofa, the cast of *Geordie Shore*, about the delights of vajaz-zling (I still have absolutely no idea what that is), he leant over to me and whispered, 'I've spent twenty-two years building a squeaky-clean television image and it's all gone down the pan in forty-five minutes.' One of the more quirky pairings that worked was John Prescott and Noel Fielding. Although they had very little in common, not least in the wardrobe department, they got on really well together.

Running alongside *Backchat* during this period, Jack had also written a sitcom called *Bad Education*. He played a hopeless teacher who was less mature than his students. It attracted a cult following among the youth and led to a feature film after the series ended. Hilary reprised her role as the mother of one of Jack's pupils, and I waited for the phone to ring. It did eventually, for the part of a priest. I would get to wear vestments, a biretta and a stole. I thought of Spencer Tracy in *Boys Town*, one of Nora's favourite films. Spencer Tracy got an Oscar for it: could there be a BAFTA on the horizon for me?

'It'll be great fun just hanging out in Cornwall for a few days,' Jack told me.

'Hanging out' was clearly an appropriate choice of words. I was called at eight a.m. and arrived in Tintagel, the location for my scene, which was set in the confessional of a Catholic church. The costume designer presented me with my outfit and then I waited to be called on set. And I waited and waited. Lunch came and went, and still I waited. Teatime came and Joanna Scanlan, my co-star in the scene, suggested we wander down to a nearby tea shop and kill some time with a Cornish cream tea. A fellow customer stopped at our table on his way out.

'You're Jack Whitehall's dad, aren't you?' he said. 'I'm a big fan of Jack's. Would you mind if I had a selfie with you?'

I obliged and he went on his way. Just as he was about to leave the tearoom, he turned round.

'May I ask you a question?' he said.

'Of course.'

'Why are you dressed as a priest?'

I explained.

I finally got on set just before six o'clock. There was a lot of frenetic activity, and an issue about how long we had left to get my scene in the can, without lurching into expensive overtime. Joanna and I had worked up some extra dialogue over tea, to give the scene more texture. The cameras turned over.

'Cut!' shouted the director. 'Sorry Michael, we haven't got time for your dialogue.'

'But Joanna and I think it's really funny,' I replied.

'No, I promise you it's much funnier, Daddy, if you just look grumpy and don't say anything,' said Jack, who had been watching on one of the monitors. 'Also, we have forty-five minutes to get the wide-shot, mid-shot and close-ups before we go into overtime.'

Charming. I've hung around, ready and primed all day, and now we have to rush through my big scene and cut all my dialogue.

A couple of months later I had lunch with Jack. As we were leaving the restaurant, he turned to me as he opened the door of his taxi and said:

'Oh, by the way Daddy, I forgot to mention, your part in the *Bad Education* movie was cut. Sorry.'

Once we'd finished filming the second series of *Backchat* for BBC 2 in 2016, Jack didn't want to continue being a talk-show host, dishing out all the best lines to his father. We did, however, think it might be an idea, at some point in the future, to do a show similar to the filmed inserts we had done on *Backchat* – teaching Jack to drive, working at B&Q and Jack taking me for a consultation with a Harley Street plastic surgeon, that sort of thing. Instead, Jack came up with the more interesting idea of a comedy travelogue.

The premise was a simple one: Jack had never had a proper gap year and – now that he had reached the ripe old age of twenty-eight – felt it was time for him to head off to the Far East. Jack had asked several of his friends to come with him on this 'once-in-a-lifetime-before-it's-too-late' journey, but sadly there were no takers; his friends were either working or married or both, and had no interest in putting on backpacks and heading off to Bangkok. And then inspiration of a sort hit him.

'Daddy, why don't you come with me to the Far East?' he said over a drink at Soho House.

'Why would I want to do that?' I replied.

'Well, it would broaden your horizons.'

'My horizons are quite broad enough, thank you.'

'And the Far East is very magical.'

'Not to me it isn't.'

'And we could spend some quality time together.'

'To be honest, Jack, I don't have a huge amount of quality time these days, and certainly not enough to travel halfway across the world with you.'

'It would give Mummy a break.'

'Your mother doesn't need a break. She's very happy living with me in Putney.'

'The money?'

'What do you mean the money?'

'Well we're hoping to do it with Netflix.'

'Never heard of them.'

'They're a streaming service. They're huge. They've got over a hundred million members. And apparently they pay quite well.'

'How well?'

'Very well.'

'When did you say we were leaving?'

And that is how *Jack Whitehall's Travels with My Father* was born.

I approached the idea with considerable trepidation. I called my trusted friend Neil to ask his advice.

'Wouldn't touch it with a bargepole,' he said. 'You know how much you hate foreign food,' he added, 'or foreigners generally, to be honest. My advice would be to give it a wide berth. If you really want to bond with Jack, bring him down to Wiltshire for a weekend. '

Heading off to Thailand and then on to Cambodia and Vietnam with someone who was forty-eight years my junior (albeit my own son) might make water-cooler television on Netflix, but it was certainly not on my bucket list. Foreign countries held little or no appeal. Travelling over Putney Bridge was adventure enough for me, or at most a villa in the south of France with twenty-four-hour access to all things English. Family and friends said I would be mad not to go, which was fine for them as I was the one going halfway across the world to be, as my mother Nora used to say, 'Made a fool of in public.'

I told Jack that I would have to clear it with Hilary.

'She won't want me to go and probably won't be able to cope without me,' I said.

I was a bit upset when I went into the kitchen and discovered that she was on the internet ordering a couple of new leather suitcases for me.

'Why are you ordering suitcases?' I asked her.

'Well, what else are you doing for those five weeks?' asked Hilary.

'I've got lunch with Neil at The Garrick Club,' I answered.

'What, and that couldn't be postponed?' She had a point. I called Jack, just to make sure he could put up with me for that long (which he rashly said he could), and signed on for what I thought might be the worst month of my life.

The furthest I had ever travelled with my own father was for a week's summer holiday in Dinard on the north coast of Brittany. I remember it being icily cold, very wet and full of British tourists in raincoats. The hotel we stayed at was run by a couple of expats; the food was English and nobody seemed to speak French. As it was my mother's idea to go there to 'improve my French', that aspect of the holiday proved to be a total waste of time. I did, however, have a chance to observe my parents on holiday, sitting in striped deckchairs fully dressed, sheltering from the rain under umbrellas, eating British food, speaking English to everyone and certainly not mixing with the natives. But that was the late 1950s. Seventy years later, would I be any different?

The plan was that we would film six half-hour shows over the subsequent four weeks. There had been a lot of toing and froing before I left, especially regarding my travel insurance; the production company had ended up paying a huge uplift on my premium to even get me on the plane. Rather annoyingly, Jack's agent had added a couple of extra nights to his comedy tour, so he would fly out to Bangkok separately. I went on ahead to acclimatise and organise my tropical wardrobe, having failed to find a lightweight suit in London in February. Travelling business class, I was not hugely impressed by the double-stalled seating arrangements, where you look into the eyes of a total stranger, or indeed any other part of their anatomy. My travelling companion was a sweaty, overweight, middle-aged man. Having travelled neither long haul nor business class for many years, I was unaware of the etiquette regarding the partition that separated the two seats and I activated it immediately after take-off was complete, only to discover that the flimsy plastic was no match for my companion's activities. He kept hitting the partition control button with his foot (having removed not only his shoes but his not entirely clean socks, revealing extremely unattractive calloused feet), which brought the partition down to reveal various other parts of his anatomy as well. At bedtime he wriggled on to his side and started talking. I thought he was talking to me so, to be polite, I lowered the partition to reveal a new tableau of horror. He was not only asleep but talking gibberish, dribbling and nursing a semi. The plan that I might arrive fresh and relaxed, having had a night in a flat bed, was sadly scuppered. At one point in the night, I escaped to go to the loo, and was pleased to see a young woman watching the start of one of Jack's *Live at the Apollo* shows. I had planned to have a chat with her on my way back and tell her that I was Jack's father but, as I approached her seat, she switched channels to the interactive flight map.

One of the biggest issues for me was the food, as I had had the odd bit of tummy trouble over the years, so eating unidentified offerings at the side of the road was not going to happen. I believe it is called 'street food'. I find anything with the prefix 'street' is best avoided at all costs – dance, art, music, but especially food. Hilary had kindly packed a small suitcase of supplies from Waitrose: Colman's English Mustard, strawberry jam, tea bags, packets of Duchy Original shortbread, tins of John West tuna, Marmite, Cadbury's Fruit & Nut chocolate and bags of KP peanuts, which turned out to be an odd choice, given that most recipes in the Far East are peanut-based and the one thing you can find absolutely anywhere there is peanuts. These supplies did prove handy on many occasions, not least when I was in local restaurants in the middle of nowhere, being confronted by an unidentified fish, smothered in chilli and a foul-smelling sauce. Jack was permanently trying to get me to try new things and embrace Far Eastern cuisine, never more so than at the breakfast buffet. I am a light breakfast man myself, liking tea, toast and occasionally a boiled egg, so I found it particularly weird in all the hotels we stayed in that these buffets covered everything from eggs and bacon right through fruit, cereal and yoghurt to deep-fried prawns, squid, noodles, rice and a full range of curries. Eating a massaman beef curry for breakfast is a very strange concept. Queueing up at these breakfast buffets whilst waiting for a lightly boiled egg, surrounded by silver dishes – some with lids – containing the foul-smelling curried offerings, reminded me of an occasion back in my early school days, when I went to stay with my friend Rothwell.

Rothwell was my best friend at prep school. I always called him 'Rothwell' because, in those days, Christian names were never used either by teachers or pupils. Even in the holidays it was 'Rothwell' rather than 'Christopher', though I am unsure as to whether that was actually his Christian name.

When Rothwell invited me to stay at the family seat in Devon, Nora spent days giving me a primer on how to behave in a stately home and packing my case (there were so many changes of clothes that I had to take a trunk). Tipping the staff, dressing for dinner, putting the lavatory seat down and using the right cutlery in the right order. Nevertheless, the one thing she failed to mention resulted in a terrible *faux pas* at the breakfast table.

First down for breakfast, I waited for Mrs Rothwell to serve up a cooked breakfast, as Nora always did in Foxgrove Avenue. When she hadn't appeared, I helped myself to a slice of toast. When she finally did arrive with Major Rothwell, Rothwell and his sister, they headed straight for the sideboard and started helping themselves to the hot food from a range of silver breakfast dishes.

'Not having a cooked breakfast, eh,' boomed the Major. 'Plenty here, old boy – eggs, sausages, mushrooms . . . the lot.'

'No, thank you sir,' I lied. 'I'm fine with toast.'

Of course I wasn't fine with toast – I was starving – but it was too late.

When I told Nora what had happened she practically went into shock. All that scrimping and saving for my education, and I didn't know the first thing about sideboards and silver breakfast dishes.

'Was there k-kedgeree?' she asked hesitantly.

Poor Nora, she so wanted to be a million miles from Beckenham.

Then it was Rothwell's turn to stay with us. Arriving at breakfast at the same time as my father, there was a brief moment of silent embarrassment as Nora led my friend across to the sideboard, which had hitherto stood in the hallway with a plant on it.

'Will you have a cooked breakfast?' said my mother.

'Yes, please,' interjected Jack.

'Well, help yourself,' replied Nora.

Jack got up and made for the kitchen.

'Where are you going?'

'To help myself.'

'But it's in the u-usual place,' said Nora, nodding toward the sideboard.

Jack strode to where Rothwell was helping himself.

'Nora,' said Jack. 'Why have you put bacon in your jewellery box?'

Nora fixed Jack with one of her looks.

'And what are the eggs doing in my silver cigarette box?'

All the effort of collecting and polishing a selection of silver boxes for breakfast had been for nothing. Jack had let her down once again. Rothwell, on the other hand, seemed hardly to notice.

I embraced a lot of things that were completely alien to me and certainly didn't feature in my everyday life in Putney – the constant heat; double kayaking (which as a non-swimmer, and with Jack in charge of the boat, was nerve-racking); Bangkok traffic in a tuk-tuk; the Khao San Road, a backpacker ghetto, my idea of hell on earth; sleeping in a beach hut, also hell on earth, and, in Phuket, a Full Moon party, beyond hell on earth. Jack had assured me that we would 'be away by midnight.' The bloody thing didn't even start until midnight, and I found myself still there at four in the morning! Fortunately, the producer had had the foresight to buy me a set of ear defenders, so I put them on and set myself up for the night in a corner of the beach with a deck-chair, a bucket of gin and tonic – yes, a bucket – and a new biography of Adolf Hitler, and left the youth to get on with whatever it is that they get on with at those parties. I didn't want to delve too much. Thailand has got the tourism industry down pat, so our first two weeks were relatively easy, especially as we were berthed in beautiful hotels. It was only when we crossed into Cambodia that things became a bit more stressful; especially when we crossed the border on foot, from rich, clean, organised Thailand into poor, shabby and chaotic Cambodia, a third world country, albeit one with big ideas and really trying to move on from its very tragic recent history and rebuild.

I found crossing the border particularly unsettling, with its beggars, noise and bustle, not to mention the horrendous smell of drains. The Cambodian border town of Poipet was extraordinary. Gambling is illegal in Thailand, so the Cambodians saw an opportunity and created a mini Las Vegas just over the border. Tall, ugly, concrete hotels lined the main strip, their sole purpose being to snare visitors into parting with their money. As you enter any of these tacky hotels, you are greeted first by ranks of security men, shortly followed by banks of fruit machines and one-armed bandits and then, finally, the casinos, three floors of vast hangar-like rooms, full of card tables and roulette wheels, packed with people duly parting with their money. The biggest problem we encountered was that due to the illegal nature of the trade, no one wants to be filmed or photographed and the casinos take a very dim view of any sort of camera equipment. This meant filming in Poipet was almost impossible.

The hotel we stayed in gave new meaning to the word gruesome. It put me in mind of what I imagined hotels in 1960s Moscow must have been like. Billeted on the fourteenth floor with a view looking back to beautiful, lush Thailand, my en-suite bathroom proudly displayed something that I had never seen before in a hotel bathroom anywhere else in the world (not that I have been to many places in the world), and that was a toilet side by side with a urinal. One for the ladies, one for the gents: very classy.

We had the services of a local guide whilst we were in Cambodia, a striking-looking character by the name of Puppet – he sported a goatee beard, wore a vest and was covered in tattoos. He was not the sort of man you would want to pick a fight with, but he came very highly recommended by the fixer we were using for the trip.

Despite his scary look, and being a man of few words, it turned out that he had very good English. It was only later that we found out he had learnt his English whilst in prison in LA. Clearly better to have Puppet inside the tent pissing out, than outside the tent pissing in. He negotiated our way around Poipet, getting us out of trouble when security waded in when we pointed our cameras at the 'wrong people' doing 'the wrong things'. He turned out to be a useful navigator too, as we drove off down the largely unmade roads further into the country. The Waitrose suitcase was going to take a hammering whilst here, I thought.

It was during our time in Cambodia that I had my first off-day. We had been filming on the Bamboo Train with Puppet all morning. Following the Pol Pot regime and the subsequent liberation by Vietnamese troops, there are still millions of land mines in Cambodia, and you have to be very careful about how you travel in rural areas. The Bamboo Train is a single-track railway that is a safe way of crossing these areas and avoiding land mines. We arrived in the middle of nowhere, so that the director could get some great aerial shots with a drone. The drone operator came highly recommended and claimed to have worked on endless Hollywood action movies, none of which I had ever heard of. No surprise there. Unfortunately, as seemed to happen often when we got involved with drones and their operators, there was a technical malfunction with his equipment.

'It's weird, because it's been working perfectly for the last forty-five minutes before you arrived,' he said as he wrestled with the now stationary drone.

'Well, if you could get it working as quickly as possible,' said our producer, 'I'd be very grateful, as the mercury is hitting the mid-nineties and I don't want everyone out in this heat for a minute longer than they need to be,' he added. So the drone man carried on trying to figure out how to rectify the problem, while we sat in the midday sun.

'What is it with these bloody techies?' I ranted to Jack as we waited. 'Every bloody time we use them, they're all great and buzzing around until you actually want them to get the shot. Fucking unbelievable.' Not totally true, but I love a rant when the going gets tough. I thought I did pretty well for the next couple of hours, but as the clock hit two o'clock, I began to wilt. Jack talked to the director on the production walkie-talkie.

'Daddy is fading fast here. You have to remember he is seventy-six; you can't keep him out in this blazing sun any more. Someone will have to stand in for him.'

The only available body was Puppet, a man whose build could not have been more different to mine. We had to swap shirts and shoes. I'm very fussy about my shoes, and watching his size 11 feet crunching uneasily into my new, beautiful, soft suede size 9 shoes – he had to squash the backs down to achieve this – was deeply depressing. He returned them to me, back in my air-conditioned people-carrier, an hour later, dripping in sweat and covered in mud. I certainly didn't fancy wearing them again but, annoyingly, continuity dictated otherwise.

Having overdone it, I felt very wan the following day, and Jack suggested that a massage might brighten me up a bit. I have never been a fan of massages, although I wouldn't have had any serious reservations had I not had a conversation with our cameraman, Nick, who had filmed a documentary there a couple of years previously. Having lugged a heavy camera around for weeks, he had ordered a revitalising massage to help with his back pain. Despite his instructions, something had got lost in translation, and he suffered the embarrassment of trying to explain to his masseuse that he did not require a 'happy ending'.

'If I do agree to a massage, Jack, you'll have to be in the room with me for the whole time. You are not to leave me alone with her at any point!'

'Isn't that a bit weird? She might think that we want her to give us a massage together.'

'I don't care what she thinks, Jack. You are not to leave me alone with her under any circumstances.'

The masseuse who arrived at my already overcrowded hotel room, Jack having taken up residence with his laptop on one side of my double bed, was not what I had expected at all. A stout woman, clearly in her sixties, with the look of a Cambodian Mollie Sugden about her; she was not the nubile temptress that I had been warned about. Her other unfortunate asset was a hacking cough, which caused her to keep leaping off the bed in order to clear the phlegm from her lungs. I was aware of Jack stifling his giggles next to me, as she pummelled away. He greatly enjoyed telling the crew at the bar later all about 'Michael's sexy massage!'

The following day Jack and I visited a monk school, where we met a group of traditional Buddhist monks. Jack taught them some colloquial English phrases. I had originally thought that they were an order of silent monks, but as Jack started writing ridiculous words on a blackboard such as banter, lash, pillock and melt (we were making a comedy show, remember), the monks started repeating them back to him parrot fashion and it became clear that they had definitely not taken a vow of silence. Before the whole process got out of control (some of the words Jack was explaining to them had become a tad risqué), we changed the subject and talked to them more generally, comparing the differences between our country and theirs. There was a serenity, innocence and unworldliness about them, which was shattered when I was sitting in our people-carrier after the filming and there was a tap on the door. Two young monks stood there smiling at me.

'Mr Whitehall, please may we take selfie with you?'

'Of course,' I replied.

I produced my phone out of my pocket.

'No, we have phones,' they said, as they peeled back the edge of their vibrant orange robes to reveal a Samsung Galaxy each.

'You very funny man. We watch you with Jack on YouTube.'

So these monks had watched us in *Backchat*?

'You on Twitter?'

'Yes.' I gave them my hashtag. And they gave me theirs. This was surreal.

'We follow you now. You tweet us?'

And there I was worrying about our risqué language.

And then off to Vietnam. Vietnam was a country that I had really only ever viewed through the prism of the war against the US. I was expecting a broken, bitter and troubled country that had never moved on from that experience. I could not have been more wrong. It is a vibrant, exciting country, one of the last communist countries in the world, but one with a layer of Western entrepreneurial spirit overlaying everything. The people are friendly and very well organised.

Through a connection of Hilary's, I had tea with the partner of the US ambassador to Vietnam in Hanoi, who confirmed my suspicions that everything was very controlled but that the government had recognised and encouraged the entrepreneurial spirit of their people and they had forged ahead. The only blind alley I found myself going up with him was when he started talking about LGBT activity in Vietnam. Where was Jack when I needed him? Unfortunately, I had misunderstood the initialism and thought he was talking about the transport system. I couldn't work out how being in a successful, high-achieving career and a same-sex relationship with two children would be an inspiring example to the LGBT community. What did this have to do with transport infrastructure? I tried a few comments about connections and rolling stock and he looked particularly perplexed when I said, 'We haven't tried LGBT in Vietnam because Jack gets very bad motion sickness. But we did travel overnight on the Eastern and Oriental Express in Thailand . . .'

'You listen to Radio Four, what the fuck is LGBT?' I asked Hilary on the phone when I returned to the hotel later.

'Lesbian, Gay, Bisexual, Transgender,' she replied. 'Why do you ask?'

'Oh God, I thought it was something to do with trains, like LNER, the train operator that used to take me back to school in Yorkshire. I couldn't work out what being in a same-sex marriage would have to do with railways.'

'Oh Michael, I hope you didn't say anything embarrassing?'

'I don't think so, but he must have thought I was mad, banging on about trains and timetables, but was clearly far too charming to say anything.'

'I suppose it would have been less confusing if he had used the full abbreviation of LGBTNQIAP+. That definitely doesn't sound like a train company.'

'What does that stand for?'

'Lesbian, Gay, Bisexual, Transgender and Two Spirited, Non-binary, Queer and Questioning, Intersex, Asexual, Pansexual and other marginalised orientations/identities,' she said.

'Oh, you're making this up now.'

'I promise you I'm not. But it certainly would have prevented the confusion. How was the tea?'

'Earl Grey unfortunately, otherwise perfect,' I replied. 'I'm going to call Neil later and see if he knows what LGBTNQIAP+ is. I bet he doesn't.'

But that encounter seemed very normal next to the strangest one of all, which involved not a local, but another visiting American, albeit one who had embraced and adopted an Eastern way of life.

In Bangkok we had received a lunch invitation from a fellow hotel guest. I must confess that I was not too sure who Steven Seagal was (I was, however, a big fan of George Segal, whose film, *A Touch of Class*, with Glenda

204

Jackson, was one of my favourite movies of the 1970s) and was certainly very hazy on his credits, but Jack was keen to meet him, having spotted him with his manager in the bar. Jack introduced himself and, before we knew it, Seagal was volunteering for a cameo role in our show. The scene would involve Jack and Seagal chatting in the front garden of our hotel before we filmed the following day. But, as it turned out, Jack asked Seagal to teach him a few martial arts moves, which prompted Seagal to fling Jack into the hotel's large ornamental pond, get into his limo and drive off, leaving Jack wet and shell-shocked.

When we returned to Bangkok, a few weeks later, his manager contacted us and invited us to have lunch with him, as he hadn't had time to say goodbye to us after our last meeting. I had my reservations, as I had found him quite eccentric but, despite his soaking, Jack was very keen to meet his hero again, so we accepted his invitation.

We arrived in the private room he had booked, to be greeted by his manager, who told us that Mr Seagal had been delayed but would be joining us shortly.

When he finally turned up, he had two young ladies in tow, neither of whom he chose to introduce, but who were placed opposite one another at the end of the table and given a glass of water. He was also accompanied by a short, menacing-looking bodyguard, who plonked himself down in front of me and ordered a black coffee. Why did the martial arts aficionado Steven Seagal have a bodyguard who was a foot shorter than him?

'Good afternoon, it's a pleasure to see you again,' said Jack, proffering a hand, which Mr Seagal chose to ignore, opting for the traditional Thai greeting of a small bow with both hands held together in front of him. This threw Jack a bit. He pushed me forward.

'Daddy, this is Steven Seagal. Steven, you remember my father Michael.' Seagal paused and then looked at Jack over the top of his shades and said,

'*Daddy?* You call your father *Daddy*?'

'How nice to see you again, Mr Seagull,' I said. He shot me a withering look as he gestured for us to sit down. As we were on a very tight filming schedule, his manager had encouraged us to order while we had been awaiting the late arrival of his client. A waitress offered a menu to Seagal to which he surprisingly responded:

'I'm not eating, thank you. I'm just here to spend some social time with these good people.'

He then turned his gimlet eye on Jack.

'So which of my films is your favourite?' A question I was glad he had addressed to Jack, as I couldn't even name one of his films, let alone pick a favourite. Jack surpassed all my expectations by describing, in great detail, a scene from his favourite, *Hard to Kill*.

'That moment when you are in the liquor store and you take on the four robbers and you get down on your knees in front of the last one standing who is wielding a knife and you break his leg by twisting his foot . . . it was brilliant.'

Steven paused for a moment.

'Yeah, I didn't like that movie. It never worked for me.'

Jack backtracked and threw in a couple more titles, to see if they got a more favourable response.

They didn't.

Seagal looked at me.

'Who are your political heroes, Michael?' I welcomed this change of topic, eager to get off Seagal's film career.

'Well, absolutely top of my list is Winston Churchill. I have all his books and a sizable collection of Churchilliana.'

'Well, this is something we share, as I am a huge admirer of Churchill too; in my opinion one of your very greatest war leaders. Some of the current lot could learn much from him. My friend Vladimir is also a great fan.' I wondered which Vladimir he was referring to, but thought it best not to enquire further. He then shared his views of various world leaders with us. He disliked Angela Merkel, Hillary Clinton and Barack Obama and was ambivalent about Donald Trump. He then swiftly changed the subject again, talking about martial arts and Samurai swords, two areas I have absolutely no knowledge about or interest in. It was evident that Seagal was clearly more of a talker than a listener, and I let him continue his lecture on Samurai swords, their usage, how they are made, the different grades of steel that can be used in their manufacture, their history, and on and on and on.

'Do you realise, Michael, that if you wanted to cut a peanut in half with a Samurai sword, you could do it in one strike? It was originally designed to take a man's head off with one swipe.' A useful piece of information for me, I thought, when next queuing at the deli counter in Waitrose.

Our lunch arrived and, with that, he pushed back his chair and stood up.

'Jack, Michael, it's been a pleasure. If you will excuse me, my PAs and I have work to do. We will leave you to your lunch.' Ah, so that's who the two young ladies were: PAs ? He swept out of the room with his entourage, leaving Jack and me in stunned silence.

I had initially said at the start of our Far Eastern trip that what I was most looking forward to was the sound of the wheels hitting the tarmac on our return to Heathrow. But when I did finally pull my luggage off the carousel (well, Jack did actually), I was surprisingly sad that our journey was over. I had met some fascinating people (and a fair number of weirdos and nutters), visited some amazing places, done things way, way out of my comfort zone and spent a whole month in the company of my eldest son. How he put up with me for all that time was probably the most amazing thing of all!

Hilary picked us up from the airport. As we sat in a traffic jam on the M4 on our way into London, I began to rant: 'Why can't you go anywhere these days without getting stuck in traffic? Who the fuck are all these people and where are they going to?'

There was a pause and Hilary turned to me and said, 'It's like you've never been away!'

As I lurch towards my eighth decade, I still have a thirty-four-inch waist, still fit into the suit I got married in, which was without doubt the best thing I ever did in my life (the marriage, not the suit), still keep Jack, Molly and Barney bemused by my extreme views on, well most things really, and always call the radio the wireless, particularly when I am talking to my friend Neil. I can text, email (up to a point), tweet, FaceTime, WhatsApp, Instagram; and although I can't swim, I try to be an early adopter but technology usually gets the better of me. I've even been to Lidl and thought their smoked salmon was excellent, unlike their clientele. I can't reverse park to save my life and have a set of ruined wheel-trims to prove it.

I'm hugely proud of my family and I hope I'll be around to meet my grandchildren, so that I can teach them important life choices, such as never serve red wine with fish, always put ladies on the inside of the pavement when walking down the street and, if wearing a hat, which I do often now that my hair is fast disappearing, always raise it when you greet people. And always write thank-you letters, preferably with pen and ink. I am hopeless at wrapping presents but rather good at writing the cards that go with them.

So, to try to answer the question I asked myself at the beginning of this book, 'What the fuck do you think you're doing?'

I suppose I was flattered that my comedian son thought his old father was funny enough to collaborate with and it would be churlish of me to turn down his offer. That, and also the fact that at my age, you don't really give a monkeys what you do, so long as you enjoy it, and I do enjoy spending time with him. Thus, a very late career as a performer was born.

Maybe Barry was right all those years ago and I am just a big show-off? And as Molly and Barney said to me, 'It'll get you out of the house Daddy and keep you young at heart.' And they were right of course. And despite my misgivings, I have obviously enjoyed this third career.

What Nora would have thought of it, heaven knows. It certainly wasn't the *à-la-carte* end of the business, more Penge than Pont Street, but at least I'd managed to hold down a job at the legitimate end of the agency business for nearly fifty years, about which I think she would have been very pleased. So why not have a go at the other end? My mother's greatest fear in life was 'being made a fool of in public'. I wonder what she would have made of her younger son doing it to himself?

Acknowledgements

Acknowledgements

The author's name on the cover of this book should in truth fall under the Trade Descriptions Act 1968 with regard to misleading consumers as to what they're spending their money on. At the risk of sounding uxorious, had it not been for the input of my wife Hilary, this book would never have been started, let alone finished. Thank you *amanuensis extraordinaire*, for your enormous help, support, enthusiasm, encouragement and sense of humour which made writing *Backing into the Spotlight* so much fun.

Thanks also to my publisher, Andreas Campomar at Constable, for having the damned stupid idea in the first place and then seeing it through: he clearly didn't learn his lesson first time around; and to my oldest friend Neil Stacy, actor, academic, medieval historian, a true polymath whose wise counsel has kept me on the straight and narrow. Likewise my new best friend Nick Hewer, who made my lifelong wish come true by inviting me into Dictionary Corner on *Countdown*. I much look forward to ageing gracefully with them both.

And most importantly to my three children, Jack, Molly and Barney, who are my reason for doing anything in life and whom I love very much. Thank you all.

Index

Index

Index